HOW TO

Climbing: From Sport to Traditional Climbing

Nate Fitch and Ron Funderburke

FALCONGUIDES

GUILFORD, CONNECTICUT
HELENA, MONTANA

FALCONGUIDES®

An imprint of Rowman & Littlefield

Falcon and FalconGuides are registered trademarks and Make Adventure Your Story is a trademark of Rowman & Littlefield.

Distributed by NATIONAL BOOK NETWORK

British Library Cataloguing in Publication Information available

Library of Congress Cataloging-in-Publication Data available

ISBN 978-1-4930-1640-2
ISBN 978-1-4930-2527-5 (e-book)

♾️ The paper used in this publication meets the minimum requirements of American National Standard for Information Sciences—Permanence of Paper for Printed Library Materials, ANSI/NISO Z39.48-1992.

Contents

A trad climber in action.

Introduction

It might be an interesting thought experiment to imagine that the climbing undertaken by an experienced, knowledgeable, and elite mountaineer is not entirely unlike the climbing we might expect to see from a four-year-old child. On the one hand, because of her expertise, the elite mountaineer enjoys a liberty that her less-knowledgeable counterparts can never understand. She is free to taste the sweetest and most elusive fruits because her skills and experience will assure her survival. Similarly, the four-year-old child is not limited by a conception of risk or peril, nor does he appreciate that the value of his endeavor is relative to other human achievements. He climbs with sublime abandon, tastes the sweetest and most elusive fruits in much the same manner. In between the sublimity of the guru and neophyte, we all find ourselves. We all strive to situate ourselves in that spectrum. We all attempt to taste sweet and elusive fruits but still make it home in one piece.

It may be helpful to think of traditional lead climbing from that point of view. It is a subject as vast and variable as the crags and cliffs we attempt to climb, and we can never know all there is to know. The mystery that lies beyond the boundary of a climber's knowledge is the most seductive part of playing in the mountains. We might stipulate, from the beginning of this text, that mystery is what motivated the first climber to climb the first thing. Novelty, adventure, and risk have beckoned to the human heart long before the invention of a sticky rubber shoes or spring-loaded camming devices (SLCDs). It bears emphasis because this text will attempt to elucidate a way to climb that is older than its nomenclature suggests. When we speak of traditional lead climbing, to what "traditions" are we referring?

In the long history of humans climbing things, our sport has grown and blossomed from its prehistoric infancy, but the first climbers of the first things still provided the framework for traditional lead climbing as we know it today. The first climbers, without a basis for comparison, tools, techniques, or precedent, started at the bottom of a thing and climbed to the top of it. The knowledge they gained from that climb informed future climbs, educated other climbers, and proved to every climber from that point forward that the mystery could be solved, that the endeavor was worthwhile, and that each objective insinuates the temptation of the next objective. Of course, today we have several millennia of human experience to inform the climber. The fruits are more elusive. Not only will each climber live and learn on a spectrum of expertise, but the sport itself is on that spectrum.

The goal here is to invite the reader to take advantage of what climbers already know. We invite you to see the cliffs and crags with the same wonder and awe as a child. The child's awe is not bound by technology or customs or comparisons, but his body most certainly is. The elite mountaineer can perceive the limits of all human accomplishment, and she hopefully will survive the nudging of that boundary. We will also try to equip you with enough expertise to be responsible and careful in the mountains, while also suggesting that limitless possibilities of traditional lead climbing are what sustain its appeal.

What Is a Traditional Rock Climb?

This text focuses on leading traditional rock climbs. While climbing might be boundless, this text must start and end somewhere. We will begin with certain assumptions about what we climb, and later we will go through the skills that a climber should acquire before starting.

To put it most simply, a *traditional* rock climb is "traditional," IF it is done on "rock," and it is a "climb."

Traditional

As we mentioned earlier, the tradition being referenced in this term is simply the idea that a climber starts at the bottom of a climb and climbs to the top, using skill, technical systems, nerve, and inventiveness to arrive there. As in ages past, the rock may or may not make the journey easy, safe, and enjoyable. Part of the tradition of rock climbing is that it is often none of those things. That is the mystery: How can a climbing team achieve a climb that proposes severe challenges? This commitment to an endeavor, to a mystery, to a great challenge is what makes the climb "traditional." It is an altogether different experience than sport climbing, or toproping, or bouldering.

Rock

Here we will narrow our focus onto small sections of rock, relatively comfortable conditions, and minimal approaches. For our purposes, traditional rock climbs are:

- Climbs that negotiate rock terrain, devoid of any snow, ice, or extensive vegetation
- Climbs that are within 1 to 2 hours hiking time from parking, infrastructure, and amenities

The climber who wishes to climb these adventurous pitches wants to experience challenge, risk management, and adventure. These climbs are a great mystery.

- Climbs that are less than 300 feet in height, and can be retreated from by walking off the top of the climb, or no more than two rappels

Climb

We wrote this text to address climbs that entirely inhabit 5th class rock climbing. There are lots of

Roan Way, in Joshua Tree National Park, CA is a great traditional rock climb. It is about 300 feet high. It is a short hike 10 minutes from the parking area. The climber does not have to negotiate snow, ice, or extensive vegetation.

different kinds of rock out there, and many of them involve intricate mazes of boulders and scree to approach their flanks. We are not dealing with that kind of climbing. We are imagining cliffs and crags where the climbing team approaches the base of the climb, climbs 5th class terrain, descends, and then quickly accesses other climbs in the same day. Many teams refer to making these kinds of climbs as *cragging*. That is our focus: cragging.

Types of Cragging

1. Base managed: Belayer is at the base of the climb the whole time. The lead climber leads, arrives at an anchor, lowers, or rappels. Someone usually goes second (aka seconds) and cleans the anchor, lowers or rappels. Climbs must be less than half of the rope length.

2. Top managed: Lead belayer starts at the base, but the second is belayed from the top, from the anchor. The lead climber leads, arrives at an anchor, belays the second up. Climbing team lowers, rappels, walks down from the top, or some combination thereof. Climbs can be an entire rope-length, but a second rope may be needed to descend.

3. Multipitch: Lead belayer starts at the base, but the second is belayed from the top, from the anchor. The lead climber leads, arrives at an anchor, belays the second up, and repeats. Leader(s) must lead more pitches to arrive at the top of the climb. Climbing team will have to make multiple transitions between safety systems going up as well as coming down. Climbs can be longer than a rope length, climbing in individual sections (pitches). **Not a major focus of this text!**

Notes on Protection

In the past, and in previous texts, the definition of trad climbing has been preoccupied with the equipment one may need to lead the climb. Sport climbs were roughly characterized by permanent protections points (requiring only quickdraws from the leader), while traditional lead climbs were characterized by removable protection points. We find these distinctions to be particularly unsatisfying, and we have taken great pains to deconstruct those ideas. Our definition of sport climb is fairly rigid, which makes our definition of a traditional lead climb fairly inclusive.

Some traditional leads may have a lot of bolts. Some may require the same size camming unit, over and over again, from the bottom to the top. The experience of protecting a lead is not our primary concern. We are more concerned with how risk management becomes the leader's primary concern, instead of simply climbing. As a result, a traditional lead climber

This protection equipment is a part of trad climbing. But, its presence on a lead is not what defines the discipline.

Sport or Trad Climb:
How Do You Figure Out?

Definitions

- Sport climbs de-emphasize risk management by managing all ground or ledge fall hazards with modern bolts.

- Trad climbs offer risk management as part of an adventure.

Climbing: From Toproping to Sport

A climb is a sport climb if:

- The climb de-emphasizes risk, adventure, and technical prowess in order to emphasize free climbing difficulty.

- The climb has permanent bolts (the type may vary) in optimal condition that are placed frequently enough to protect a climber from ground or ledge fall for the entire length of a lead.

- The climb has an obvious and permanent two-bolt anchor at the end of the route that can be cleaned by lowering through permanent rings, quick/rapid links, or carabiners.

- The climb has been largely cleared of conspicuous debris and rockfall hazards.

- The climb is not in a remote or alpine setting.

- The climb does not require intermediate belays to complete.

Resources

Refer to guidebooks or online descriptions; ask local climbers or climbers with previous ascents; and evaluate in person!

must be equipped to manage risk in lots of different ways. Our text focuses not only on the equipment needed, but on movement, decision making, conscientious risk taking, and calculating the likelihood of injury or death.

Progressions and Transitions

A common progression is to learn toproping and beginning climbing movement in a climbing gym, transition to outdoor toproping, and eventually learn to lead climb. The lead phase of this progression commonly starts with sport climbing in a gym, then moves to sport climbing outside. Many, but certainly not all, will choose to continue by learning traditional lead climbing skills outside in single pitch setting, followed perhaps by multipitch traditional climbing. On the surface, trad climbing seems well defined and manageable. In reality, defining a trad climb, building the necessary physical, technical, and mental skill sets, as well processing all the risks present to utilize sound judgment, is a sometimes overwhelming task. Trad climbing, as we define it, hosts a substantial portion of the world's climbing terrain, and mastery of this discipline permits access to a lifetime of both challenge and adventure.

Why Trad Climb

Trad cragging is fun with physical, mental, and technical challenges. Much of this additional focus and challenge results from leading and placing protection. This climbing discipline provides access to a variety of "topless" cliffs and it's a gateway skill set to many multipitch routes.

Trad climbs can look like many things: Crack and face climbs with great protection opportunities, splitter cracks in the desert, runout slab climbs, multipitch slab routes with bolts or fixed protection, face climbs without many bolts, and many more.

Assumptions about prerequisite skills are needed to move forward. We know what sometimes happens when you assume, but in order to focus on the skills necessary to transition from sport climbing to single pitch trad climbing, we need to assume the reader has the skill set outlined below. We simply cannot discuss all the necessary skills for a climber who wants to learn to trad climb. We will focus on those required to move from a sport climber to a trad climber. We ask that you take personal responsibility to ensure moving forward is a task for which you are prepared. There will be some review of these assumed skills and contextualization of general climbing best practices and sport climbing best practices in chapter 1. The focus of this text is presenting skills and procedures for trad leading. If these prerequisites are not in your skill set, check out our other works or find an experienced

Assumptions and Prerequisites Transition

- Savvy toproper technically and physically
- Savvy sport climber technically, physically
- Possess basic climbing technique on slabs, face, and cracks
- Belay, knot, and anchor skills for toproping and sport climbing
- Knowledge of basic equipment and its use per manufacturer's specifications
- Knowledge of natural, artificial, and fixed protection (see *Climbing: Protection*)

climbing mentor or American Mountain Guides Association (AMGA) professional to help you.

These foundational notions on trad climbing allow this text to move forward more clearly and address its primary mission: to help a sport climbing leader with a well-rounded set of protection skills manage and enjoy this subdiscipline of climbing and transition to leading single pitch trad climbs, cragging variations, and perhaps multipitch trad climbs. This is a common progression of growth for many climbers. What skills from sport climbing are needed to become a trad climber? What skills are unique to trad climbing? A set of technical and risk management skills and the necessary trad leading skills will be addressed.

This book has several missions:

- To confirm and review assumed prerequisite skills and general climbing and sport climbing best practices

- To cover the basics of trad climbing and some of its variations

- To help readers increase risk management, and to expand the terrain to be safely explored and enjoyed

- To aid the reader in transition from a sport climbing leader to a trad leader through an introduction of necessary skills, best practices, action steps, and a plan to successfully meet this goal

- To encourage *personal responsibility* and self-assessment

CHAPTER 1

Review of Assumed Skills: Toproping, Sport Climbing, Protection, and General Climbing Best Practices

One of the most common explanations for accidents and mishap in American climbing is cited as "exceeding abilities" by the renowned American Alpine Club annual publication *Accidents in North American Mountaineering.* The common thread in so many accident narratives involves a climber who was willing to take enormous risks without enough prerequisite knowledge to manage those risks.

There are common themes to this kind of presumptuousness. The climber didn't think that a fall was likely. The climber was misusing unfamiliar equipment or climbing in an unfamiliar environment or situation. The climber didn't anticipate an unexpected circumstance or occurrence. We would be willing to stipulate that in each case, the climber probably didn't know what they didn't know. Many climbers get injured in this fashion and would have benefited from learning more before attempting a traditional lead climb.

Because American climbing provides so many different disciplines, rock types, styles, and subcultures, many American climbers do not always appreciate the interconnectedness of each discipline. American trad climbers, in particular, admire and hold dear the purity of their discipline. As a result, a certain propensity to eschew sport climbing, toproping or bouldering, or indoor climbing can be observed. But that kind of insularity often results in a lack of appreciation for interconnected disciplines.

For example, a trad climber must appreciate that even the most mundane trad climbs have cruxes. Bouldering, sport climbing, toproping, and indoor climbing help a climber hone their free-climbing abilities, so that cruxes can be tackled with a practiced panache. Sport climbing teaches a climber to take and catch lead falls. Bouldering trains a climber to take short falls, develop body control in the air, and quickly negotiate amorphous ground-fall zones. Toproping familiarizes a climber who is anchor building with natural protection components, fixed protection components, and perhaps even removable artificial protection. Meanwhile, traditional lead climbing teaches a climber to climb a line of weakness, a slab, and an odd-sized crack. It also teaches a climber patience and preparedness with a diverse and voluminous skill set as well as an appreciation for adventure. All disciplines of climbing inform and enhance each other.

This book stipulates that there is an appropriate time and place to start learning to lead trad. There is an appropriate progression to acquire skills while taking and managing risks responsibly. In modern climbing, we believe that a logical progression starts in the gym with learning to toprope. Then, toproping outdoors is a logical way to diversify and expand one's skill set. After some time toproping, learning to build anchors, interacting with a community, and caring for the climbing environment, leading climbing indoors and sport climbing outside are logical pursuits. Finally, after learning to lead in these environments, where risk management is de-emphasized, it might be appropriate to learn to lead in an environment where risk management is central to the enjoyment of the pursuit. Adventurous trad climbs, by their nature, allow climbing teams to flirt with expansive and sophisticated risk categories. If that flirtation comes at the expense of one's wellness, or even one's life, it doesn't seem prudent or fun.

What common skills and best practices from toproping and sport climbing do you need to become a trad climber? Which ones are unique to trad climbing and which ones are needed to be fully prepared for trad climbing? The answers are not always simple or clear. Starting with the toproping and sport-climbing skill sets outlined below will assure a climber is ready to build a trad climbing skill set. Chapter 2 outlines new skills and best practices a trad climber must embrace to start their journey.

Relevant Toproping Skills to Traditional Lead Climbing

We assume that the reader has spent some time toproping and learning a minimum skill set before experimenting with techniques explored in this text. Toproping is one of the best ways to learn foundational rudiments like movement, anchoring, and

Do you know these knots, hitches, and bends?

belaying. Toproping teaches a climber to belay, to tie knots, to move on the rock, to be outside responsibly, and to use climbing equipment. We assume that readers have learned the following skills from their toproping experience:

- Environmental and cultural norms common to American crags, including Leave No Trace (LNT) practices, stewardship, and how to interact with a climbing community.

- A selection of ropework techniques, including stacking and managing a rope, knots, hitches, and bends. More specifically, we assume a climber knows the following knots and hitches: figure 8 follow through, figure 8 on a bight, overhand on a bight, BHK (Big Honking Knot), bowline, bowline with bight, flat overhand, double fishermen's, clove hitch, Munter hitch, Munter-mule-overhand, mule overhand on an MBD (Manual Braking Device), Prussic, autoblock,

COPE Acronym

- What is the **C**ONTEXT of the ropework?

- What are the **O**PTIONS?

- Selection is based on the **P**ROS AND CONS of the available options.

- **E**XPERIMENT with the selection and reflect on better solutions.

Kleimheist. We assume that the reader has learned to COPE with each of these knots and hitches.

- A working knowledge of common climbing equipment: helmet, harness, shoes, chalk, belay devices, locking and nonlocking carabiners, ropes, anchoring hardware, cords, and runners. Use, care, and retirement per the manufacturer's specifications. All the necessities for being outside comfortably and safely.

- The fundamental principles of belaying and how those principles are applied to MBD and ABD (Assisted Braking Device), including correct setups, inspections, double checks, and communication. We assume that the reader is a competent belayer in any toprope setting.

- A basic understanding of climbing movement on slabs, cracks, overhangs, and face climbs. Trad climbing allows the leader to climb many pitches that might never have been equipped for sport climbing, but it is advisable for the aspiring trad leader to have learned to climb at least at the 5.6 level on a toprope.

Can you build this NERDSS toprope anchor and manage risk while doing so?

- A command of the fundamental principles of anchoring: strength, redundancy, appropriate load distribution, minimizing extension, and simplicity (NERDSS): No Extension, Redundancy, Distribution, Strength, and Simplicity. Speed: For trad climbing an extra *S* for *speed* may be a valid emphasis, as trad climbing can be a slow discipline due to the physical and technical challenges. We assume readers know how to use a 4-foot sling, a cordellette, and/or a section of static rope to build anchors.

- A working knowledge of toprope belay system that includes examples for a variety of crag types, an understanding of the fundamental principles of belay, setup and double checks, belaying and lowering, the use of an ABD and an MBD, arresting a fall, and communication.

- How to rappel with an extended belay/rappel device and a friction hitch backup.
- An understanding of best practices for general climbing applications and risk management, backups and double checks, closing the system, site use, belaying, rappelling, and anchoring.
- Personal responsibility in the above areas, acceptable use of climbing resources, and emergency preparedness.

Relevant Sport Climbing Skills to Traditional Lead Climbing

We assume that you have learned a few skills that are most easily and safely acquired in a sport climbing environment. Sport climbing gives sport climbers the task of additional risk management by asking them to lead climb, and the dynamic nature of that environment prepares the leader for traditional leads in a way that few classrooms can duplicate. Sport climbing teaches a climber to lead belay, the fundamentals of leading movement (like avoiding tripping, clipping, resting, and falling), how to clean anchors, and how to do more thorough research for a climbing outing. We assume you have learned the following skills from your sport climbing experience:

- How to research a climb and seek objective, subjective, and consensus data. We assume you have grown accustomed to using that data to pack your bags, select equipment, and be prepared for contingencies. We assume you know the difference between a sport climb and trad climb, and plan accordingly based on the data gathered.

- How to belay a leader with an MBD and an ABD, including paying out slack, compensating, catching falls, and providing just the right amount of "softness" to a catch to make it as comfortable as possible for a lead climber. We also assume you know when and how to use a ground anchor as a lead or toprope belayer.

- How to lead climb while managing the rope, avoiding tripping hazards, correctly clipping the rope at increments, and resting on the rope when necessary.

- How to take lead falls of manageable length.

- How to build and clean anchors by lowering off of a variety of fixed anchor types, primarily, and how to do so by rappelling when lowering is not possible or acceptable.

- An understanding and utilization of best practices for sport climbing applications.

Relevant Protection and Anchoring Skills to Traditional Lead Climbing

The anchors you learn to build in toproping, and through a continuous exposure to the sport, teach a climber to evaluate naturally occurring components like trees and boulders. But we assume you will have been exposed to artificial components as well. It will be difficult to learn to trad climb without a working knowledge of permanent fixed artificial components and removable artificial components. We assume you will apply the knowledge gained while building toproping anchors and sport climbing to traditional

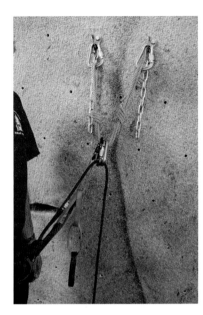

Can you build this anchor on a fixed anchor and clean it later to retrieve your equipment and manage risk while doing so? (small opening fixed anchor with a Quad anchor on it)

lead climbing. That means that we assume you are familiar with evaluating and utilizing:

- Natural protection like trees and boulders.
- Fixed protection like modern mechanical and glue-in bolts, and pitons, including evaluating them for signs of corrosion, age, and instability.
- Artificial removable components:
  - SLCDs (aka cams) including the camming range suggested by the manufacturer and evaluating rock feature and quality for appropriate application.
  - Chocks, stoppers, and nuts, including how to recognize constrictions in the rock where their placement is both secure and reliable,

RADSS: A Tool for Assessing Artificial Protection

Rock quality
Appropriately placed

The 5 Rights

- *Right Size:* A proper fit. Bigger is generally better.

- *Right Place:* Best spot in that area. Ask yourself if it could be better if moved slightly, adjusted, put deeper/shallower, flipped over, etc.

- *Right Piece:* Correct type for rock configuration (parallel, constriction, etc.). Cams are generally in parallel places, nuts in constrictions.

- *Right Way:* Per manufacturer's guidelines.

- *Right Removal:* Easy to get out.

Direction of pull
Surface area
Symmetry of placement

RADSS guidelines inform a rating score and the proper utilization of individual pieces.

4— "Textbook," picture perfect. Confident it *will* hold forces of a lead fall.

3—High quality/solid and secure. Piece *will most likely* hold forces of a lead fall; not quite "textbook," but close.

2—Low quality/marginal. Piece *may* hold forces of a lead fall, but is uncertain/unreliable.

1—Poor quality. Piece will hold body weight only (if that!); *will not* hold forces of a lead fall. *Do not use in an anchor!*

and evaluating rock features and quality for appropriate application.

- Tricams, including how to apply them to flares, pods, and pockets that may not be conducive to other types of protection, and evaluating rock features and quality for appropriate application.

- Hexes and other forms of protection based regional nuances and specific sites and routes.

- Attaching to these protection components, with ropes, slings, quickdraws, and cordage.

What If These Prerequisites Skills Are Not Available to the Reader?

This book might be valuable without the skills mentioned here. It might enhance planning or give a better sense of direction with learning if you know what you are trying to learn prior to too much hands-on practice. However, we think the skills mentioned here best prepare you to learn the craft of traditional lead climbing, and we strongly encourage you to consider the information in this text theoretical until your practical experience makes use of it.

The previous books in this series (*Climbing: Gym to Rock*, *Climbing: Protection*, *Climbing: Knots*, and *Climbing: From Toproping to Sport*) can be helpful, especially when accompanied with supervised, cooperative, and supportive mentorship. If informal mentors are unavailable, the services of an AMGA-certified climbing instructor or guide might be the most accessible way to get the practice you need before getting the most out of this book and trad climbing. If nothing else, ground school exercises can give you a risk-neutral platform for skill acquisition.

These prerequisites are just a start. If you are not there yet, reading this text can still be an edifying experience, but it will probably not be practically oriented. For practice, you will need an effective safety net to help you fill in the gaps, so it is advisable to seek additional instruction and mentorship to accompany this book.

These students are learning to place trad gear, evaluate rock, and remove gear on a boulder. Better to learn on the ground rather than 100 feet up.

An AMGA-certified guide or climbing instructor can devise curriculum, and find great learning venues and activities to give practical experience.

Planning and Preparation

A trad outing involves so much more equipment than sport climbing, toproping, or bouldering that one of the first things a trad climber must learn to do happens long before traveling to the cliff. Research, planning, and preparation are heralded rituals for any adventurer, and it is no less important for a trad climber.

Planning and preparation for a day of trad climbing involves many considerations: research about the location, the necessary technical skills, and the required equipment. There may be difficult route finding, a lack of fixed of anchors, long approaches or returns, and a whole host of information that, if ignored, could ruin the outing. But, the amount of information available can be confusing, so it is helpful to sort the information into three categories: objective data, subjective data, and consensus data. Each of these data points has corresponding considerations in terms of required equipment and materials, so it is important to know what data to look for and what to do with data once you have it.

Finding Information

Guidebooks. The most current edition is most valuable. Any text that is more than ten years old is likely to have many inaccuracies.

Open-source databases. Open-source databases can be very helpful. But the information offered to an open-source website, especially in the form of comments and photos, can be subjective and distorted by the contributor.

Local beta. Local climbers and guides often have lots of information, and they are usually happy to share. The researcher must sort out objective and subjective data.

Joshua Tree guidebooks.

Savvy trad climbers in action, employing best practices and possessing a well-rounded skill set.

Objective Data

Objective data points are valuable, and they are indisputable. They include the following:

- **Route length.** The total length of a climb is a crucial data point. A lead climber will need enough rope to complete the entire climb, or a plan for how and where to segment the climb.

- **Anchor type.** A lead climber will need anchor-building equipment, so it is helpful to have a rough idea of what the anchor(s) on a climb are. Each anchor can require slightly different equipment, and the leader needs to know what to bring along to build them.

- **Features.** The features on a climb directly affect the equipment the lead will need. Certain features like roofs and wandering face climbs require extra slings or a double rope lead-climbing system.

- **Crack sizes.** Traditional lead climbs often take advantage of cracks to place removable protection, and the range of sizes available on the lead translates into the rack that will accompany the leader: Big cracks require big gear; small cracks require small gear. It is often unnecessary to carry every size if the available placements do not vary and are consistently big or small. Oftentimes a "standard" rack is carried with a range of protection types and sizes.

- **Protection frequency.** There is no need to carry a lot of protection if there is a dearth of placement opportunities. It is similarly avoidable to have too few options when placements abound or the pitch is long. Unlike sport climbing, the trad leader often has more control over protection frequency.

When climbing a single crack feature for example, the leader might place protection every foot, but he will need to carry many units.

- **Descent.** The mode of descent—how one gets down from a climb—is another vital data point. Typically, the team either walks down from the top, in which case walking shoes (and a way to carry them up) may be required in addition to climbing shoes. Or if the team rappels, another rope may be needed.

- **Retreat options.** At any given time, the climbing team should know their retreat options. For shorter climbs, the leader can be lowered to the ground, and the gear can be abandoned until it can be recovered in the future. For longer climbs, the team should know how to retreat to nearby ledges or rappel stations, create bail off rappel stations, or join other parties.

Guidebook representations and descriptions of a climb are some of the most basic attempts to record objective data.

Objective Data Summary

Objective data	Typical options	Equipment needed	Skills needed
Route length	≤ 300-foot-long climbs for the techniques in this book.	If the route length exceeds half the rope length, a second rope may be required.	Longer routes may require expert anchor building, extra stamina, additional ropework skills or rappelling.
Anchor type	Trad anchor, bolted anchor, other fixed anchor, natural anchor (tree, boulder, thread).	Removable protection to lead and build an anchor, anchor building materials (4-foot sling or cordelette), carabiners, and belay devices.	Anchor building skills and stance management; top belay skills; rappelling may be required.
Features	Cracks, corners, faces, slabs, roofs, and combinations of features.	Slings and extensions may be required to keep the rope line from creating too much rope drag; a second rope may be needed.	Appropriate rope line management; additional ropework skills, i.e., double rope technique.
Crack sizes	A physical measurement of the crack size is the most objective; some cracks are a consistent size, some vary.	Removable protection to protect the entire pitch in that range.	Jamming, use of camming devices, how to haul a pack in a wide feature.
Protection frequency	Varies according to feature; cracks have a limitless frequency, but slabs and faces may have large gaps between placements.	Enough protection to create the desired frequency (e.g., 100-foot climb requires 10 placements for a 10-foot protection frequency).	Ability to assess fall consequences and protect against it.
Descent	Rappelling, walking, lowering and cleaning.	Shoes, a second rope, rappelling equipment and anchor cleaning tools.	Climbing with a pack, rappelling, anchoring, and cleaning.
Retreat options	Lowering, rappelling, walk offs.	Equipment that can be abandoned.	Knowledge of all retreat options on any given cliff.

Subjective Data

Traditional lead climbing can be quite variable, and each climbing team has the freedom to solve lots of different problems in lots of different ways. It's difficult to create entrenched value judgments when so many options are both efficient and relatively safe, depending on climbers' skills and abilities. One climber may decry the risks she perceives on a given climb, while another thinks the risks are reasonable. Risk doesn't have an absolute value, nor does difficulty, nor does challenge. It's all relative to the climber. As a result, traditional climbing is full of subjective data that is only valuable when filtered through the perspective of the source. Subjective data includes the commitment grade, the strenuousness, the quality of the protection, the rock quality, and the protection rating.

- **Commitment grade.** The commitment grade generally refers to how difficult retreat would be, or, more generally, how long it would take a "typical" party to complete the route. Grade I is single pitch. Grade II is a two or three pitch climb/couple hours. Grade III multipitch/full day. Grades IV and V grand wall and multipitch/long day or more than one day.

- **Strenuousness.** The strain climbers exert might be entirely relative to how fit they are, how quickly they find and place protection, how their movement skill set matches that required by the route, and how strategically they rest or distribute their body weight.

- **Protection quality and rock quality.** When lead climbers place protection, fall, and rip the protection out of the wall, or when they break holds off, it is difficult to blame the incident entirely on the rock or the protection. Maybe the climber should have inspected the rock more carefully before pulling or standing on it, or when placing protection behind it. Maybe the protection was located poorly or incorrectly. One climber's choss heap of loose rock is another climber's monolith, so evaluating both rock and protection quality should be at best an average of knowledgeable and experienced opinions with misinformed or naive opinions.

Subjective Data Summary

Subjective data	Range of possibilities	Relevant questions
Commitment grade	Grades I to VII (this book does not venture further than Grade II).	Do I have enough equipment and time to complete the climb?
Strenuousness	Stances between every move to no stances at all. Movement skills required?	Do I have enough stamina to deal with placing gear while tired/pumped?
Rock quality	Brittle to solid.	If the rock is brittle, is there a way to avoid the brittle parts?
Protection quality	Adequate or inadequate; there is nothing in between.	Is the inadequacy of the protection a shortcoming of the protection, the rock, or the climber's abilities?

Consensus Data

When enough people agree that a subjective value is the same, it has a consensus value. When one climber believes that a climb is 5.10 but one hundred climbers believe that it is 5.11, the opinion of the one climber is essentially obfuscated, no matter who that climber happens to be. The *Yosemite Decimal System (YDS) and Protection Ratings* tend to function in this way. The most prevalent YDS difficulty and protection rating tends to have the authority of consensus behind it.

The protection rating is often the most subjective bit of information. Roughly, G climbs have good protection. PG is pretty good. PG-13 is pretty good but may be nuanced or a little bit tricky to place. R means that the route has significant portions of unprotectable

Yosemite Decimal System (YDS) Grades

How 5th class movement (what most think of as roped rock climbing) difficulty ratings are clarified in the United States:

5.0–5.4: Minimal difficulty; beginner level

5.4–5.7: Moderate difficulty; beginner/intermediate level

5.7–5.10: Advanced difficulty; experience needed

5.10–5.15: Expert difficulty; experience and specific training needed

Note: This scale can expand as more difficult climbs are completed.

Other Grades

Plus and minus signs (+/–) are given to routes to denote difficulty, for example, 5.9+ is more difficult than 5.9–.

Letter grades (a, b, c, or d) are sometimes added to a route that is a 5.10 or higher grade to indicate shades of difficulty; for example, 5.10b is more difficult than 5.10a.

Protection Grades

Protection grades are given to indicate the ability to protect a climb.

G—Protection is good and always available.

PG—Protection is good but not always available.

PG-13—Protection is adequate but needs to be carefully managed.

R—Protection is present but long sections of the climb may be unprotectable. There is groundfall potential.

X—Protection is minimal and long, severe falls are possible. Groundfall or ledgefall is almost certain.

climbing, and X means that protection is so infrequent that a fall would be catastrophic.

Ratings of G, PG, PG-13, R, and X have a linear arrangement, but their absolute values cannot be pinned down. How good does protection have to be to be G? How runout does a pitch have to be for R? What is the tipping point between PG and PG-13? There are no answers there. The best we can do is refer to general consensus of other climbers.

Consensus Data Summary

When it comes to YDS or protection ratings, the range of possibilities are established. What are the relevant questions: What are my abilities? Is the local concensus different from other areas? Do I know and can I see where and why someone decided to give a certain protection rating?

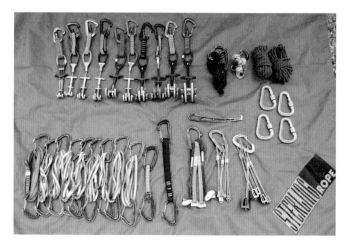

"Standard rack" and equipment needed for a day of trad climbing.

After a climbing team has done adequate research and planning, preparations can be made in terms of required equipment, itinerary, goals, and contingencies. If climbers don't take the time to gather information before an outing, odds are they will not be prepared to have a fulfilling experience at the cliff.

Visual Mapping

Once all the information about a given climb has been gathered, it is wise to find a place, usually on the approach, where there is a vantage point over an entire climb. It is not uncommon to witness a climber "mapping" a climb from this vantage point. The aspiring leader has trained his eyes to see the cliff through the eyes of a lead.

When visually mapping, be sure to:

- Forecast the movement.

- Assess the protection possibilities and the anchor location: Is the type of anchor known?

- Get an idea about which stances will be best for placing protection.

- Find any undesirable hazards that the climb might pose and develop protection strategies.

- Realize inherent hazards if both belaying and climbing are not set up and performed correctly.

- Determine the type of climb and terrain access: single pitch or multipitch, belay(s) location, walk off, lower off, or rappel off?

Leave No Trace

The Access Fund's Rock Project has been doing a superb job of educating American climbers about caring for the nation's crags. Asking all climbers to make a pact to preserve the resource and our sense of community is something climbers shouldn't need, but as more climbers misbehave in the mountains, it's clear that each individual must make a personal commitment to care for the resource. Before climbing, consider the main points of such a pact: Respect other users. Dispose of human waste properly. Park and camp in designated areas. Stay on established trails. Place gear and pads on durable surfaces. Clean up chalk and tick marks. Keep a low profile; minimizing group size.

Equipment

The equipment needed for a successful trad climb-ing outing can vary from one location to the next. The number of pitches and terrain access are huge considerations here. The entire retinue of trad climbing equipment, regardless of location, stems from an emphasis on managing risk. As a result, the team that has grown accustomed to packing for sport climbing or toproping outings will be able to leave some things at home but will need an entirely new set of tools. If the terrain dictates longer approaches, or the base is not to be returned to, or there are other needs on the route to be considered, your equipment needs become more complex. Whatever you bring, know what you have, what it is made of, and how to use it per manufacturer's specifications.

Backpacks

Depending on the climb, you may need in your quiver a small lightweight backpack to wear while climbing and a larger backpack for getting to a site where you return to the base. Be careful with sizes. A large backpack will inevitably be filled with items the team might not have packed if the space was unavail-able. Similarly, a pack that is too small will result in unpackable necessities dangling from every loop and strap. Or, the team will make unnecessary sacrifices simply because of the backpack. Carry just what you need for the objective at hand and select a backpack that holds it.

Rope

Trad climbs can wander, have low-angle terrain, feature disjointed planes of rock, and have sharp protrusions. There are ledges and edges to be wary of. Ropes can rub against all these features, not to mention a falling leader can bang into them if the rope elongates too much. The application of a thinner rope to abrasive terrain is unwise. A "beefier" 9.5mm to 10mm diameter rope with a lower elongation will likely serve you well in the rigors of trad climbing.

How long should a trad climbing rope be? A prudent leader should know how long a climb, lower, and rappel are, and how long the rope is before climbing. The savvy trad climber knows this information before arriving at the climbing site.

Harness

Trad harnesses should balance comfort, weight, and capacity. Padded legs and waist—norms for most harnesses—are important for a harness you may be in all day and one that is weighted down by all the gear racked on its gear loops. Adjustable legs and waist allow flexibility when wearing different clothing combinations. The ability to carry part or all of a trad equipment rack, in addition to the equipment your harness normally holds, is important. A trad harness should be a workhorse that can carry a lot of equipment, adjust to clothing combos, and be comfortable.

It is recommended that you try on and hang in a harness, loaded with equipment on it, before buying. It is also recommended that you try it while carrying equipment, in the style you have or will develop (e.g., runners on front gear loops, belay device, anchoring material, accessory cord on back gear loops, etc.).

Shoes

It is advisable, depending on the nature of the climb, to purchase the best shoe for the job. Because trad climbs and feet are so diverse, we really cannot steer you too much toward a particular type or style. However, certain shoes perform better in certain situations, such as edging, jamming, all-day affairs, smearing, and so on. Try to pick a relatively comfortable all-around performer if you are just starting out and plan on investigating a broad array of climbs. Choose specialized shoes as you plan particular adventures on routes with distinct movement characteristics.

Helmets

In trad climbing, helmet use is more common than in other disciplines of climbing. We dare say it is a norm, although we know this is not the case, especially with single pitch trad climbing. Make a very careful choice if you ditch the helmet. In the event of an unexpected rockfall or dropped equipment, both more common when trad climbing, a helmet can mean the difference between a thrilling war story and permanent disability or even death.

Rack

The rack is one of the signature features of trad climbing. Its presence on an outing often categorizes the goals and the expertise of the entire team. It can be an unwieldy assembly of equipment, and many climbers accustomed to toproping or sport climbing have to adjust to climbing with extra weight and tools. The components that compose such a creation are not typical or standard. A rack's composition really depends on the climbing area, the user, and the specific use or route. Guidebooks will sometimes define a standard rack for an area or route, and local climbers will certainly have their opinions and advice on this topic. Despite the variety, all racks tend to serve two main goals, and it is therefore helpful to organize them that way. All racks should allow a leader to (1) protect an entire pitch and build an anchor with removable components or attachment tools (slings and cordellette); and (2) anchor, belay, descend, and deal with contingencies. As a result, we will divide all racks into two main parts: a protection rack and a tool rack. A protection rack has all the slings, carabiners, runners, quickdraws, and removable protection the leader will need to protect a pitch or build an anchor. The tool rack consists of all the belay and rappel tools, anchoring tools, and accessories.

Protection Rack

The protection rack consists of all the tools the climber will need to lead a pitch, but not necessarily everything the climber will need to anchor or belay or solve problems. It's just the lead climbing gear. The protection rack consists of the protection, the attachments/extensions, removal tools, and extra carabiners.

PROTECTION

- **Passive:** nuts (aka chocks, rocks, stoppers); shaped metal that is wedged into the rock

Protection (L to R): Passive (nuts), hybrid (tricams), and active (SLCDs).

- **Hybrid:** Tricams and hexes; shaped metal that is placed in such a way that rotation occurs to further jam the component in the rock; also can be placed passively (similar to nuts) and wedged into the rock

- **Active:** Spring-loaded mechanical devices (SLCDs) that expand when force is applied and further jam the component in the rock. Many kinds: big, small, rigid, flexible, three-cam units, off-sets, and cams with large expansion ranges.

- **Specialized:** Big Bros, ball nuts, removable bolts, and more; specific designs and functions with limited utilization

ATTACHMENTS AND EXTENSIONS

The following definitions can add some clarity to understanding soft goods (aka textiles) used as attachments.

- **Sling:** a sewn or tied loop of a flat textile (nylon, spectra, etc.). Shoulder (standard) length and double length are common. Some protection, such as Tricams and spring-loaded camming devices (SLCDs), have an integrated sling.

- **Runner:** a sling with two carabiners, one on each end. The sling used to make a runner is usually shortened via passing the carabiners through each other in a particular manner. When done properly, you can unclip any two strands to extend back to full length.

- **Quickdraw:** a rigid or semirigid textile with two carabiners, one on each end. One of these carabiners is typically held in place tightly to facilitate clipping.

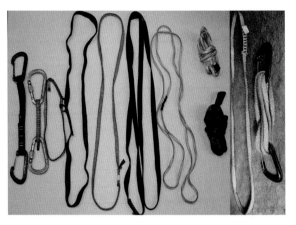

L to R: Quickdraws, slings, and a runner.

Be conscious of sewn joints (bar tacks) and knot-ted joints in these attachments. Ideally they are kept off of components and carabiners and are not in any new knots that may be created. Also beware of quick-draw accessories (usually some sort of rubber) that help stabilize the clipping carabiner. These have been misused with tragic results. Ensure that carabiners are properly through the quickdraw's soft good material, not just the rubber stabilizer.

REMOVAL TOOLS (AKA NUT TOOLS, CHOCK PICKS, ETC.)

These are used to help clean the removable artificial protection common to trad climbing, out of the rock's cracks and fissures. This tool is a must for the second to carry. Nut tools are typically necessary in order for them to complete their cleaning duties. Many leaders also carry a removal tool. Occasionally a leader will get a piece of protection stuck that they would like to remove to adjust or use elsewhere. This leader's nut tool can also be a back up for the team's seconding duties. Oftentimes some sort of small "keeper cord" is tied to a nut tool. This allows it to be clipped to the climber or the system in some fashion to prevent losing the tool due to drops. Some will carry these with the protection rack and others with the tool rack.

EXTRA CARABINERS

A handful of extra carabiners are common on most protection racks. A few nonlockers or various configurations come in handy when extending, retreating, dealing with gate interference, combining protection placements, or building anchors. A few locking carabiners are also helpful when retreating, dealing with gate interference building anchors, or constructing locker draws.

Two non-lockers create the security of a locking carabiner.

Non-locking Carabiners into Locking Carabiners

Two non-locking carabiners can be used together with gates opposite and opposed to create an improvised locking carabiner. This technique may be handy to improvise a locking carabiner to utilize in a critical application/ link. There are only so many locking carabiners a climber will carry.

Tool Rack

Trad climbers typically need a few more tools with them. Anchoring, belaying, and contingencies all must be dealt with on the climb, and therefore those tools should be accessible at all times.

Anchoring tools will be needed on a trad climb. It is conceivable that a trad climbing team may position itself on one anchor and lead to another anchor; therefore the team will need more than one cordellette or 4-foot sling to build the second anchor. Two cordellettes and two 4-foot slings usually allow teams enough versatility to deal with any anchoring sequence. Additionally, locking HMS or pearbiners allow the

Anchoring attachment tools: The cordellette and 4-foot slings allow a leader to deal with any sequence of anchors that may arise. Notice how the materials are compact and bundled. Gloves and locking carabiners are helpful when anchoring and then top belaying.

leader to anchor the climbing rope with a clove hitch at any time.

Belay and rappel tools are also a part of any tool rack. There are only a few different ways that trad climbers belay, and the devices vary accordingly. Trad climbers belay at the base of a climb, like sport climbers and topropers do, so everyone in the team needs a good tool for belaying a leader, like an MBD or an

Left: Devices to belay a leader: MBD, ABD, and Pinch/ extra-grabbing. While many trad climbers have all three options on their tool rack, some prefer to pick and choose and travel lighter. Right: Devices to belay a second: Plaquette, ABD, and Munter hitch.

ABD, or an extra grabbing Pinch device. Trad climbers also belay on top of a climb, off the anchor; there are a few belay options for that arrangement as well: ABDs, plaquettes, and the Munter hitch. Teams have lots of options if they become accustomed to having all these devices at their disposal, but every option might not be needed on every climb.

Accessories are also needed on trad climbs for a variety of emergency preparedness tasks, retreating, backups, and creature comforts. They can include rap rings, gloves, a knife, a nut tool (seconds should always have a nut tool), a spare belay and/ or rappel tool, and an accessory loop(s) for friction hitches.

Accessory bundle: These tool rack accessories are often bundled together on one carabiner since they are not always needed, but they're always nice to have.

Belay Device Comparisons

Belay device	MBD	ABD	Munter	Plaquette	Extra grabbing plates, aka Pinch devices
Belaying a leader?	This works great for belaying a leader so long as the belayer is perfectly attentive and uninjured.	An ABD increases impact forces on protection, but provides a margin of error if the belayer is inattentive or compromised.	This is an ideal belay technique when belaying off a fixed point; otherwise it can be awkward. Not great for lead belaying.	This works like a regular MBD when belaying a leader.	An extra grabbing pinch increases impact forces on protection, but provides a margin of error if the belayer is inattentive or compromised.
Belaying a second off the anchor?	A poor choice: The braking plane makes it difficult to give a fundamentally sound belay off the anchor.	This gives a smooth and reliable belay. It also quickly converts to hauling, to give assistance.	It works great for belaying a second so long as the belayer is perfectly attentive and uninjured.	This is great for belaying off the anchor, if the belayer only needs to take in slack continuously.	While these devices will work, the operation is not as smooth as the alternatives. Can be complex to rig.
Lowering?	Easy to lower a leader, but lowering a second off the anchor requires special redirects and rigging.	Easy to lower a leader, but lowering a second off the anchor requires special redirects and rigging.	Easy to give a smooth lower, but a friction hitch backup is usually advisable.	Easy to lower a leader, but lowering a second requires intricate redirects, backups and rigging.	Easy to lower a leader, but lowering a second requires intricate redirects, backups and rigging.

Belay device	MBD	ABD	Munter	Plaquette	Extra grabbing plates, aka Pinch devices
Rappelling?	Great for rappelling. A backup is a best practice.	Can only rappel a single strand. Requires knot-block or counterweight techniques for rappelling.	A poor choice for rappelling. The reversal of the brake strand twists the rope. A backup is a best practice.	Works like an MBD for rappelling. A backup is a best practice.	While these devices will work, the operation is not as smooth as the alternatives. A backup is a best practice for most.
Take it or leave it?	The regular MBD is less useful for trad climbing; a device that can also serve as a plaquette is more versatile.	If the weight and size is not a problem, an ABD is a great tool in any trad climb.	HMS and pearbiners are needed for a variety of applications. The Munter is always an option for the things it does well. (Belay second off an anchor and lower climber from a top anchor.)	Take it. Modern plaquettes require special knowledge, but they are incredibly versatile.	If the performance deficit between this device and its alternatives is not too distracting, it can be very versatile. A great backup device, too.

Organization and Racking

Once a rack is selected and assembled, it has to be transported to and from the venue, and at some point a leader has to climb with all that equipment, too. How does one carry all the components of the protection and tool racks? There are as many different ways of organizing equipment (racking) as there are climbers. It is a highly personal system. The key is for each individual to develop a system that is comfortable, compact, efficient, organized, and effective for the applications at hand. Some options are described below.

Organization for Transport

When stowing all the equipment in a backpack, there are a few organizational options. The rack components can be consolidated in a variety of ways on carabiners, a gear sling, on separate slings, or on the harness and then stowed inside. Many climbers find it difficult and cumbersome to transport equipment on the harness, because the harness is difficult to put on when laden with equipment. Many climbers keep their tool racks on the harness at all times, but the protection rack is carried separately. And many climbers empty every item off of the harness and utilize a backpack before and after every climb and outing. The rack components are often carried on a gear sling over the shoulder and outside of a backpack, depending on approach length and individual tastes.

Organization and Racking for Leading

Once the rack has been transported to the cliff, the leader must disperse the protection rack and the tool rack in a way that makes the tools instantly accessible, does not encumber the climbing, and is also easy to reorganize for subsequent leads. Again, there are many variations, alternatives, and hybrid strategies, and any given climber may use one system for one climb while varying it altogether for another climb. But here are the main strategies: rack on a sling, rack on a harness. Within those strategies, climbers further delineate between grouping components on a single carabiner to dedicating a carabiner to each component individually, as well as in combinations or with other organizational methods. It is a very personal system that is well-thought out and developed over time.

LEAD WITH RACK ON A GEAR SLING

Some or all equipment is racked on a sling that is worn over the shoulder.

Pros

- It's advantageous when the leader needs to carry a large volume of gear or large protection units.

- It's advantageous when the entire body has to be wedged in a large crack or chimney—all the equipment can be shifted from one side to another.

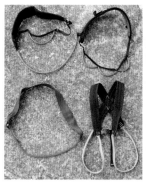

Gear slings for racking.

A racked-up gear sling.

- It's quick to hand off to another leader and easier to see/inventory all components in one glance.

Cons

- It's more likely to drag or get stuck on the rock, especially on slab or face climbs.
- Weighted sling may not be as comfortable for smaller amounts of equipment. On overhangs, sagging sling is not always agile or accessible.
- It does not work well for all body types.

OFF THE HARNESS

Everything is clipped to the gear loops on the climber's harness.

Pros

- Equipment is more accessible.
- For smaller racks, it can be more comfortable to carry the equipment.
- Especially nice on slab or face climbs.
- It's more agile and accessible.

Rack on harness: This climber is racked on the harness, an ideal arrangement to lead a low-angled face, to lead with small rack, and for some climbers on all terrain. Note the runners over the shoulder.

Cons

- It's more time-consuming to hand off the rack to another leader.

- When the climber's body is mashed against the rock, the equipment on that side of the harness is pinned against the rock.

- It's more difficult to see/inventory all components in one glance.

HYBRID

This is a little bit of both. It could either take the best of both worlds or make a disorganized mess. Typically climbers using this style will rack runners and the tool rack on the harness, and the protection rack will be on gear sling over the shoulder.

Other Considerations

There are two that may affect your racking choices. The first is physical comfort: What system is more comfortable, and how long will you need to carry it? What is your application? The second is center of gravity: When climbing, the rack's mass can affect your center of gravity. This has some correlation to gender but is individual specific.

Using Racking Carabiners

Components need to be attached to the gear sling or harness via carabiners. There are four variables to consider:

1. How many components per carabiner (one or many)?

2. In which direction will the carabiner be clipped (gate facing in or out)? (Everyone has a preference.)

3. What order or system will be used for the protection components (by size, big to small or small to big; by type; or by both size and type, for example)?

4. How will the protection be utilized and what attachments need to be added?

A strategy that allows the climber to select the protection size and type needed in a smooth, quick, and efficient manner is the standard. Before (and sometimes after) achieving this standard, many climbers will rack so that they have immediate alternatives on a multicomponent racking carabiner. Putting multiple components on one carabiner becomes cumbersome with big components. It also becomes time-consuming when the nature of a climb allows the rope to be clipped and attached directly into a component; if a component does not have its own carabiner, it must be placed, unclipped from the others, and then reclipped with an extra carabiner or runner. Consider racking single-piece carabiners when pieces do not look as though they need to be extended (e.g., in a straight up-and-down splitter crack). People also rack in this manner when the climb is short, hard, or has limited protection.

What Happens to the Runners, Slings, and Quickdraws?

Again, there are many choices for a leader to consider when deciding where to carry these attachment tools. Some like to carry them on the harness, other climbers like them on a gear sling, and still others carry them over the shoulder. Many of these choices depend on style. Most of the time quickdraws and runners (aka alpine draws) are carried on the harness. Some climbers use only premade runners and quickdraws, and rack them on a gear sling or harness. Some climbers use slings that go over the shoulder and some free carabiners when climbing (in conjunction with any of the racking methods above). These are then utilized as attachments when necessary. Regardless of quickdraw, runner or sling preferences, it is common for a couple of double-length slings to be carried over the shoulder as part of a rack to be used for a variety of reasons (natural pro, rope drag, anchor building, etc.).

Typical or "Standard" Rack

The components that compose such a creation are not typical or standard. A rack's composition really depends on the climbing area, the user, and the specific use or route (e.g., are you setting multiple

A "standard" rack. Always keep it clean and organized, in good working order, and out of the dirt!

toprope anchors or leading a wide crack?). Guide-books will sometimes define a standard rack for an area or route, and local climbers will certainly have their opinions and advice on this topic. Most climbers start with a protection rack composed of a set of nuts minus the smallest three or four sizes and a set of cams minus the very small and very large sizes (smaller than fingers, bigger than fists), perhaps with some doubles, and some Tricams (pink, red, and brown are popular). Ten to twelve runners or quickdraws, and a couple of double-length slings round out the protection rack. A nut tool and a cordellette as well as a tool rack and necessary accessories are also considered part of a "standard" rack.

All these aspects of organization and racking are important to consider. This should be a deliberate process that includes individual tastes and informed actions. Practice is the key. Try different racking meth-ods on climbs you are comfortable on or when mock leading (practice under a separate top rope belay) to determine what works for you. Use the information here and try racking choices on all different types of climbs. The goal is to come up with a system and process that works for you and helps you be organized and racked effectively to aid in risk management and maximize your climbing experience. Experiment and practice.

Trad Ropework

T he ropework used in traditional lead climbing has slight nuances and variations that are not always obvious to climbers accustomed to sport climbing and toproping. The biggest difference is that the traditional lead climber will often belay on the top of a pitch, which has immediate ramifications for the stance and ropework. First of all, unlike toproping or sport climbing, the belayer will want to be anchored the whole time when he or she belays on the top of a pitch. Second, the belayer will need not only to be in a position to belay, but he or she will have to manage the rope while belaying. This management is truly important for any post belay action. Third, lowering or rappelling from the top of a climb requires a slightly different application of friction hitch backups and joining knots than those learned while toproping or sport climbing. Lastly, the knots and hitches used to function, manage risk, and deal with emergencies are more consequential when the climber and the belayer are both hanging in a dangerous place at the same time.

Anchoring Ropework

When a traditional lead climber arrives at the belay site at the top of a pitch, she will build an anchor and then attach herself to that anchor in order to relinquish the lead belay, pull up and start managing the rope, and belay the second. The clove hitch is one of

Climber attached to anchor with a clove hitch, belaying a second. This climber's application of the clove hitch allows him to stand securely wherever he likes on the ledge. He has adjusted the hitch to allow himself to lean back on the anchor and supervise the second climber.

the most common and versatile ways for her to do so. The clove hitch is quick to tie and adjustable, and it allows the leader transitioning to become a belayer stand in whatever position allows her to belay effectively, to do ropework, and to supervise and communicate with the second.

Stance Management

Using clove hitch or other acceptable connection to the anchor, the stance must have one guiding principle—to provide an effective belay. This consideration should be first and foremost. Comfort is secondary, although the savvy trad climber finds ways to have his cake (a good belay) and eat it too (comfortable stance). The stance should ensure:

- An effective belay. Slack management and braking are easy to perform.

- Good sight lines and communication. Can you see and communicate with the second?

- Good rope management. Can you easily transition to lowering, rappelling, or other action without any tangles or rope messes?

Rope Management

Standing on a tiny ledge while belaying requires the traditional lead climber to keep a growing pile of rope tidy and well organized. In toproping, climbers learn that keeping the rope in a neat, concise pile is a good way to keep the climbing site organized. In sport climbing, a neatly stacked rope allows the belayer

Rope stacked neatly on a small ledge This rope is perfectly manageable, and the belayer will be able to keep it that way once the second arrives at the anchor.

Rope coiled across the belayer's lap at a hanging stance. When there is no ledge or feature to work with, these lap coils will suffice. But it takes careful back-and-forth coiling to maintain organization, as the coils can be difficult to hand off to another belayer or manage in the next lead belay. Making coils progressively a bit smaller helps prevent tangling.

to feed rope to the leader without interrupting the leader's progress to solve problems.

In trad, those obligations are no less important, but finding available space to do so can be challenging. The rope should either be stacked neatly at the belayer's feet, or neatly coiled across the belayer's lap if ledges and features are unavailable.

Backups

Lowering a second from an anchor requires ABDs and plaquettes to be redirected to maintain the necessary control of the brake. Plaquette devices and Munter hitch lowers can be secured by using a friction hitch backup. Using a friction hitch to back these types of lowers is a best practice. These lowering precautions are not reinforced during a day of toproping or sport climbing, and they are easy to forget.

The brake strand must be redirected before opening the GriGri's (or any ABD's) braking cam when lowering.

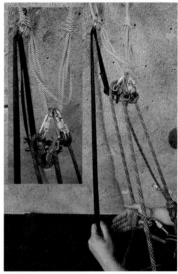

If the belayer disables the blocking function of a plaquette, the brake strand should be redirected and an autoblock backup applied.

Lowers from the top belay with a Munter hitch feel more secure when an autoblock backup is applied.

Joining Knots

Trad climbers are likely to join two rope/cordage ends in contexts where the joining knot could be consequential. Long rappels, for example, will require a climber to join two rope ends and load the joining knot during the rappel. The three options and their ideal application are: 1. Double fishermans: Joining rope ends that do not need to be untied, like accessory cords and cordellettes. 2. Flat overhand: Joining two ropes of similar diameter (≤1mm difference) for rappelling; beware joining greatly different diameter ropes with this knot. 3. Butterfly: Accessory cords, cordellettes, or ropes.

Managing Problems

When belaying at the top of a trad climb, the lead climber and the lead belayer should be prepared to deal with problems. The lead belayer may need to tie off the leader. The belayer on the top of pitch may need to tie off the second.

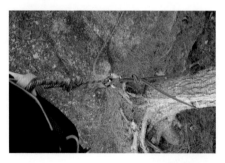

Belayer tie-in closes system. Because the belayer is already tied in while he belays (and clipped to a bottom anchor), the system is closed and he can quickly transition to climbing once the leader is ready to belay from above.

Munter-mule overhand (MMO). The top belayer can use the MMO to tie off the second if he or she elected to belay with a Munter hitch.

GriGri with catastrophe knot. The top belayer can use an overhand on a bight to confidently secure an ABD or a plaquette.

Lastly, because the leader will often lead, anchor on the top of a pitch, and belay, she may not always be in view of the second when he begins to climb. Furthermore, the leader may need to lower back to the ground unexpectedly from high on the pitch. Here it is advantageous for the second climber to tie in before the leader begins leading. This habit closes the system, allows both climbers to check each other's knots prior to the lead, and also provides an easy way for the belay to ground anchor if necessary.

Mule overhand on an MBD. The lead belayer can use the mule overhand to secure an MBD and tie off the leader. There are two methods to complete the mule: one on the carabiner's spine (left) and one above the belay device (right)

Best Practices

Y ou are going trad climbing! Your preparation and research have led to navigating successfully to the climb's base—now what? In traditional lead climbing, the climbing team will need skills that are not necessarily reinforced by toproping or sport climbing. Some climbs are so long that the lead may need to belay from the top of the climb, bring up a second, and then either lower or rappel or walk down from the top. A second rope may be needed, or perhaps walking shoes to hike to the bottom of the cliff.

In this chapter, we will explore the basic structure of the crag: the base, the protection and anchors, and the top. We will also explore the best practices and governing strategies for each of the segments of the climb. The context of these is variable depending on the type of trad climb:

- Is someone staying at the base the whole time—base-managed cragging (classic single pitch)?

  - Lead climb and be lowered

  - Lead climb and rappel back to base

- Are you both leaving the base and returning—top-managed cragging (classic single pitch and walk-off single pitch)?

  - Lead climb and top belay

  - Be lowered one at a time (one lowered from top and one lowered from base)

Summary of Trad Crag Structure and Process

Section of the crag	Variations and options	Decision points
The base: The beginning. Sport climbing and toproping prepare a climber to recognize the base. But in trad, these sites may be harder to find and organize as well as use.	Flat and open. Heavy vegetation. A steep hillside. Talus, rocky, ledges.	Locker room: Where are we going to put our stuff? Ground anchor: Will we need one? Lead belayer: Where will the lead belayer stand and if appropriate anchor?
Protection and anchors: The middle. The "middle" of trad crag can have enormous variety. Sometimes there is a lot of protection, other times little; sometimes permanent anchors, sometimes none.	Protection rack: number and style of components, runners. Tool rack: anchoring and belaying tools. Removable components, permanent components. Natural components.	How much rack will we need to create the protection frequency we want? Will we need certain protection components, attachment materials, and tools and not others?
Top: The end. The precipice, the summit, or simply where the team decides to stop climbing; the top is not always the literal top.	The summit of a tower, dome, or feature. The spot where the rock face rejoins a hiking trail along the top of the cliff. The last permanent anchor the team reaches on a given climb.	Will we need anchoring and belaying tools for consecutive pitches? Will we need another rope to rappel? Will we need to shoes to walk down? Will we need food, water, extra clothes while we climb?

- Rappel
- Walk off

- Are you both leaving the base and not returning (walk-off single pitch and multipitch cragging)?

  - Lead climb and top belay

- Sometimes repeat—multiple ascending pitches of lead climbing and top belaying back to back

  - Rappel to a different locale
  - Walk off to a different locale

- Are you both leaving the base and returning after multiple pitches (multipitch cragging)?

  - Multiple ascending pitches of lead climbing and top belaying back to back
  - Rappel back to base
  - Walk off back to base

The big plan consists of clear answers to the following questions:

- What do we need to carry with us or do with our stuff?

- What do we need to be prepared for the required technical skills and physical motion?

- How are we communicating (verbally, visually, or using rope gestures)? What commands are we using?

- Do we need any other equipment (e.g., approach shoes for a walk off?)

- Where are we going? Where are we going to end up? How do we get down?

A Trad Climbing Belayer Should:

- Give the climber constant and complete focus during all phases of a lead climb.

- Ensure preclimb checks are thorough and performed.

- Assess if a backup belayer or bottom anchor is needed.

- Spot a climber prior to the first protection placement when necessary.

- Remain aware of the fall path of the climber.

- Move rope out of the climber's way during spotting phase or during initial part of climb.

- Never let go of the brake strand of the rope.

- Constantly manage the rope so it is smooth. efficient, and effective with just the right amount of slack. during leader movement and clipping.

- Can brake and hold a lead fall at all times.

- Prepare with a stance and location to do so—position of function.

- Realize comfort and location is secondary to the necessity of maintaining a good belay for the leader.

- Lower a climber in a safe manner.

- Help the lead climber in risk management.

The Base

What happens at the base? LNT concerns are prevalent because the base of the climb is a comfortable place to take care of bodily needs, such as food, water, and bathroom. Helmets are usually worn. Equipment is racked, organized, and stowed. Also, members of the climbing team separate into their respective roles, and all the minute preparations for leading and seconding are made. The trad climbing team consists of a leader and a belayer (aka the second), and they may alternate roles. The base of the climb is the last opportunity for the climbing team to consolidate their "Big Plan" before things start getting too treacherous and confusing—what to carry, how to communicate, where you are going, and how you'll get down.

The Base

Climbing team member	Roles and responsibilities
Belayer (second)	Helps coordinate the Big Plan, flake or stack the rope, closes system and ties in, sets up lead belay (device, stance, bottom anchor, spotting), and gives an interactive lead belay. Communicates, observes, and assesses leader's risk management, climbs, and removes all protection from the pitch.
Leader	Helps coordinate the Big Plan, racks and gears up, ties in to climbing rope, maps climb (first omnidirectional piece, movement and protection, rope path and extension, anchor), leads the climb, manages risk, anchors and belays the second, communicates.

Protection and Anchors in the Middle of the Climb

While the leader leads, the belayers belays; then the leader becomes a top belayer and the original belayer becomes a second, climbs, and cleans protection. Those moments are the main body of the trad climbing event. Every climb will pose its own challenges, and many climbing teams will have to learn to manage risks that may not always have easy solutions. But every team should strive for the following best practices:

- Lead climbers should have a thought process and plan in place.

- Lead climbers should bring and place enough protection to protect the leader from ground or ledge fall, if possible. Eschewing placements that could protect a leader from ground or ledge fall is unnecessarily risky.

- Every placement should be capable of sustaining all the potential loads applied to it: lead falls, outward pulls, lifting rope action, and so on. Omnidirectional placements are usually most secure and are a must for the first protection placement of the climb.

- The rope line should be as straight as possible.

- All fixed protection components (bolts, pitons) in the rock should be briefly inspected before use.

- All anchors and belays should be fundamentally sound.

- Seconds should remove all protection from a pitch, striving to leave nothing impermanent behind.

Protection Thought Process

- Is there a need? Why?

- Location: Where and when can I meet that need?

- Application: What can I use to meet that need, and how?

Omnidirectional

This is perhaps the most important component of a protection system when lead climbing. The omni-directional is a protection component that needs to remain secure in any possible direction of pull. Many combinations of components and attachments can be utilized for this application. Omnidirectionals are necessary to maintain the integrity of the whole protection system. This first component should protect against a ground fall (or factor 2 fall when multipitch climbing) if a fall were to occur just above it and before other components could be added ("down" and "out" are typical pull directions). It also needs to withstand upward and greater outward directions of pull resulting from a fall higher up (with additional protection components in place), which tensions the rope all the way to the belayer, causing up and out forces on this important first piece.

If the first piece is not omnidirectional, it can be compromised and fail, as can other components in the climb after this initial failure. This is the *zipper effect*, where the components unzip out of the rock all the way to the one component that was just fallen upon. One can imagine the terror of being high up on a climb, hanging from one single piece. Omnidirectionals also may be needed throughout a climb that has large or wide ledges. The rope tensioning process will repeat, and the potential of unzipping unidirectional pieces occurs again.

Some examples of omnidirectional components include:

- Stable, nonwalking SLCDs, especially those placed in a horizontal crack

- Natural components (e.g. trees, threads, radical horns, or other rock features/components) that can withstand strong multiple directions of pull

- Nuts (or other unidirectional components) in opposition

- Extremely slotted passive hex, nut, or tricam

- Tricams (active) can be multidirectional, especially when placed in slotted horizontal cracks

Omnidirectional.

The Top: The End of the Climb

The top of a trad climb could be a setup and rigging at existing fixed anchors commonly used for descent, or it could be a walk off after some removable artificial anchor or natural anchor. The top could also be some other point that the team elects to retreat from. If rappelling, the climbing team will be conducting one of the most accident-prone activities in trad climbing. Lowering a climber also has risks. Once the actual leading and seconding is complete, teams can become too relaxed and complacent, but lowering and rappelling have the same stakes as climbing. It is important to stay focused and attentive.

The following best practices should be considered at the top of a climb:

- Manage personal risk and create a NERDSS anchor.

- Choose a belay device and setup that is best for the site/application—be deliberate!

- Lowers from the top of a climb should be backed up. If the belayer releases the brake hand, the lower should be instantly arrested by some form of backup.

- Rappels should also be backed up; if the rappeller releases the brake hand, the rappel should be instantly arrested by some form of backup. They should be managed: Is the middle of the rope at the anchor so that equal length strands stretch down the pitch? Does it reach where we want it to? Get us where we want to go? They should be closed: Close the system—tie knots in each end. Overhands on a bight are great.

- Rappel ropes should run through a smooth metal surface, like rappel rings or carabiners, so the ropes can be pulled from below. Avoid rappelling directly from vegetation to protect bark, roots, and soil.

- Walk offs are more comfortable in walking shoes.

- It is almost never necessary to toss rappel ropes.

- Closing the system is especially important when lowering and rappelling.

Top Belays

In this and our other books, we have focused on belaying at the bottom of a cliff. Top belays, or belaying from the top of a cliff or pitch, are an essential skill for trad climbing. With the exception of the classic single pitch trad climb found in base-managed cragging, where one member of the climbing partnership is always at the base, top belays are necessary and required. When both climbers are leaving the base, or when one returns later (or not at all), the top belay is employed. Situations like this could occur when climbing in top-managed cragging and multipitch cragging outings. Bottomless cliffs, those with no or limited bottom access like Acadia National Park's Otter Cliffs, are also often accessed via a top belay.

The biggest difference between top belays and the belays customary in toproping and sport climbing is that the top belay is directly off the anchor. The belayer's own body weight is not used as a counterweight. Rather, the second's body weight is directly assigned to the anchor at all times. Interestingly, this arrangement often places less overall force on the anchor, since the load is not doubled by a counterweight. It also allows the belayer to multitask: manage ropes, maintain a brake hand, offer assistance, rerack, and manage the stance.

The top belay can also be set up with an MBD/ABD direct off the harness's belay loop, and redirected from the harness's belay loop through the anchor. We

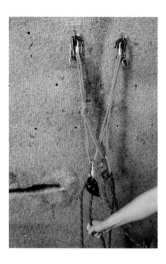

A great top belay: An ABD setup direct on an anchor.

acknowledge these methods can sometimes be applied correctly and safely, but for simplicity, consistency, security, and overall management of a top belay, we feel belaying directly off the anchor is the way to go. **We strongly discourage the other methods in most top belays.**

In this chapter, we will explore the use of the ABD, the Munter hitch, and the plaquette as ideal top belay tools. Each device has slight differences in the way it converts to lowering, how it is backed up, and how it is tied off. But the movement of rope and the application of the fundamental principles of belay are the same with all three devices. In each segment, we will stipulate that the belayer is anchored with a clove hitch and that the master point of the anchor is chest-to-eye level. These high master points are ideal for top belaying. The other tasks implicit in that arrangement (anchor site selection, rope management, and stance management) have already been briefly discussed and will be discussed further later.

Less than Optimal Top Belays

- Using an ABD or MBD on the harness. The climber's rope is redirected through the anchor's master point and down to the climber.
  a. Commentary
     i. This works in a similar fashion as a bottom belay in a typical base-managed cliff bottom toprope situation.
     ii. Twice as much force is put on the anchor, but this is not usually a concern.
     iii. Belayer can get sucked toward the anchor and pulled off his stance if a fall occurs.
     iv. Assuming the stance isn't compromised, lowers are relatively smooth and straightforward, but still require a backup.
     v. It's a moderately complicated process to go hands-free at the belay.

- Direct off the Harness
  a. Use an ABD or MBD direct on the harness; the rope goes from this belay point directly to the climber. (The belayer, as in all top belays, should be smartly anchored.)
  b. Commentary
     i. Beware the ABC (anchor-belayer- climber) line that will straighten out in the event of a fall. Will this pull you or compromise your breaking ability?
     ii. This is not recommended unless you want or need the body to absorb forces.
     iii. This is the most complicated process to go hands-free at the belay.

Obviously there are pros, cons, and serious considerations to weigh for each. Again, we advocate a direct off the anchor top belay. It is the most ergonomic and has the most practical applications and flexibility.

Munter hitch and plaquette top belays direct off the anchor.

Common Direct-Off-the-Anchor Top Belay Errors

Munter Hitch Belaying Errors

- Set up in a twisting or rubbing manner

ABD Belaying Errors

- Assuming assisted braking is automatic and hands-free. It is not.
  - Rope has to be correctly inserted and within the correct diameter range for the device. Even when within the manufacturer's usable range, skinny-diameter ropes perform differently.
  - Light climbers can affect the assisted function.
  - Rope drag and rope friction routes can affect the assisted function.

- Light hangs (not falls) may not engage the cam.
- Lowering too fast and loss of control.
  - Lowering without a redirected brake strand.
- Brake hand is removed without a catastrophe knot or system close.

Common Plaquette Errors

- Incorrect setup or connection to anchor.
  - Lowering too fast or loss of control.
- Lowering with an incorrect procedure (per manufacturer and best practices).
- Pulling too tight on climber/ inability or incorrect slack giving.
- Brake hand removed without a catastrophe knot or system close.
- Rope inserted incorrectly—load strand goes on top of brake strand or closer to anchor's master point.
- Inappropriate rope diameter for device.

Taking Rope In

Whether using an ABD, a Munter, or a plaquette, the belay mechanics are the same. The brake hand must never let go of the rope, the hands should only transition when the rope is in the brake position, and the hand and limbs should be positioned comfortably and naturally.

Sidestroke Belay Mechanics for a Direct Top Belay (Munter Hitch, Plaquette, or ABD)

Step 1: Spread out the hands. The brake hand starts near the belay device on the brake strand, the other helper hand reaches down the climber's strand.

Step 2: Pull down on the rope with the break hand and up on it with the helper hand.

Step 3: Complete the sidestroke—"put the apples in the basket"—the hands meet near your midsection —"the basket."

Step 4: Pinch the brake strand below the brake hand and slide the brake hand back up the rope to the belay device. Don't let go of the rope with the brake hand!

Step 5: Reset and spread the hands out again.

Step 6: Repeat steps 1 through 5 until the climber reaches the anchor.

The sidestroke top belay method.

Lowering Off the Anchor

Lowering a climber from a top belay can be smooth and comfortable, but when executed imprecisely, it is often time-consuming, cumbersome, and unnecessarily dangerous. For all three belay techniques, the rope should be stacked neatly beneath the belayer's brake hand so that it pays out smoothly into the lower. Many lowers are encumbered by poor rope management; the belayer should be able to lower the climber smoothly. There should be an adequate backup. The belayer should be prepared at any time with the tools and knowledge to employ the proper lowering technique an entire rope length back to the ground or last multipitch anchor.

When lowering any distance with an ABD, the brake strand must be redirected (see photo on page 58). Once the camming mechanism on an ABD is deactivated with the lever, the belayer will need the friction of the redirect to keep the brake strand in the braking plane. It will be nearly impossible to give an effective lower without the redirect. Even with the redirect, smooth lowers take practice. If the belayer is incapacitated, the ABD is likely to lock and arrest the lower, so no further action is needed to back up the ABD.

When lowering with a Munter hitch, a friction hitch backup (such as an autoblock) should be applied to the brake strand of the hitch and connected to the belayer's belay loop with a locking carabiner (see photo on page 58). As the belayer lowers, the autoblock is kept in hand and tended/not allowed to grab. If allowed to engage, the autoblock will tightly grab the brake strand, so it should be kept loose and used solely as a backup. If the belayer becomes incapacitated, the autoblock will engage and arrest the lower.

Lowering with a plaquette is a much more complex arrangement, and doing it smoothly requires considerable practice. In plaquette mode, the belayer does not even have the option to lower the climber. So, if a lower is to be achieved, the belayer must rearrange the plaquette, and that requires some assistance from the climber. We do not advise the use of a plaquette if a climber is likely to need slack or lowers while seconding a pitch.

Before a lower, a small amount of slack can be given with the "rocking" technique. This technique may be necessary for too tight a belay. This is often witnessed in trad climbing when this over-tightness sucks a second into a piece of protection they are about to clean, thus limiting their cleaning effectiveness. The plaquette does not intuitively or easily remedy this situation. To give small amounts of slack, the belayer can gently and slowly "rock" the rope blocking carabiner up and down. This is not a pull out and is not forceful, but merely a shifting of this carabiner back and forth. A few "rockings" should give the second enough slack to continue cleaning. This is not a technique for lower of any substantial distances and with a practiced plaquette belay, should not be necessary. It is worth repeating: We do not advise the use of a plaquette if a climber is likely to need slack or lowers while seconding a pitch.

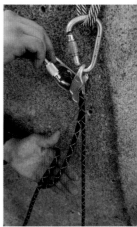

Small amounts of slack can be given by slowly rocking the rope blocking carabiner. Be cautious and maintain control of the brake strand!

For a lower of long distance (as far as back to the ground or last anchor) or when substantial slack is needed, the plaquette needs to be converted into essentially an MBD style device.

To convert a plaquette to a lower, the belayer must execute the following steps in the following order:

1. Redirect the brake strand through the shelf of the anchor or the master point with a locking carabiner.

2. Apply a friction hitch backup to the brake strand; an autoblock is a good one. Connect this hitch to the belayer's belay loop with a locking carabiner.

3. Connect a double-length sling to the lowering hole of the plaquette or the blocking carabiner and redirect it with a carabiner through the shelf of the anchor or the master point.

4. Pull the sling down (it may need to be extended with another sling or stepped on) and tend autoblock to lower; this will rotate the plaquette in an MBD-style mode. This can be abrupt, so be careful.

To halt the lower, let the autoblock grab the rope and ease off the pull on the sling. The device should

The setup to lower a climber when top belaying with a plaquette.

return to plaquette mode. A backup knot like an overhand on a bight can enhance security on the transitions.

Tying Off the Belay: Baseline

In some circles, tying off the belay on an anchor and going hands free is known as *baseline*—a good place to be or get to for incidents and emergencies. When using a Munter hitch, the mule knot, and overhand backup (aka MMO) allows the belayer to relinquish the brake strand (see photo on page 63). That knot should be familiar to trad climbers.

The ABD and the plaquette use an aggressive braking mechanism (the ABD's cam and the plaquette's rope blocking and pinch) to supplement the belayer's brake hand. But fundamentally sound belay practices require the constant and vigilant use of the brake hand no matter what device the belayer is using. With an ABD or plaquette, a simple overhand on a bight knot in the brake strand provides an adequate backup. But that knot should be within a few inches of the device.

The plaquette pictured here is secured by an overhand on a bight, also known as a catastrophe knot. An ABD can be similarly secured with an overhand on a bight (see photo on page 63).

CHAPTER 7

Anchors

B uilding advanced and complex anchors, beyond building natural component anchors when toproping or building fixed component anchors when sport climbing, is a fundamental part of trad climbing. These anchors are commonly composed of artificial removable components (and sometimes natural components). One of the assumptions of this text is familiarity with and skill building anchors using natural and fixed components. We assume the reader remembers the fundamental principles common to all anchors. All anchors have the same basic parts: protection components, attachments, and master point to consolidate the utilization.

Anchors should be built deliberately with the NERDSS principles (see page 18).

Traditional lead climbers' anchoring skills become inherently more complicated when seeking to apply the fundamental principles of anchor to more complex scenarios. For example, building an anchor on a pair of bolts, or three good cams, for toproping is fairly simple. It's simple because the anchoring tools are all available, and the direction of load is always in one direction. But a traditional lead climber attempting to establish a top belay is dealing with a much more complex scenario. If the leader has depleted his or her rack by placing lead protection during the climb, he or she may be forced to build an anchor with whatever protection components remain on the rack. Limited resources always require more innovative techniques. Also, top belays may require an anchor to be loaded in many different directions. An anchor may be loaded by the belayer in one direction, leaning back on a clove hitch. It may be loaded by a falling climber in a different direction, toward the last piece of protection. It may be loaded by the climber and the belayer in various directions as they climb, manage their stance, fall, lean, or lower. This results in tugging and loading from different directions. Or the anchor may be loaded in an upward direction by a lead fall on a subsequent pitch. The leader's anchoring skills and awareness must be sophisticated enough to deal with all of these possibilities.

As a result, we will divide anchoring skills into two categories: simple and complex. Simple anchors deploy the same tactics, techniques, and tools in toproping and sport climbing. Complex anchors are more rare, but they certainly occur with enough frequency that a leader cannot afford to ignore them. Complex anchors are needed when leaders are constructing anchors with depleted resources and directional variability—multiple directions of loading. Regardless of composition, all trad anchors should be composed of evaluated and appropriate components—of greatest importance is the individual protection component, which should be evaluated by RADSS and score well by these measures:

- Adhere to NERDSS and have a functional well-positioned master point (chest to eye high).
- Be in line with the desired climb and direction of pull resulting from falls (lead and toprope).
- Keep the belayer stable, secure, and in a functional position to provide a proper belay at all times.
- Should not fail.

Anchor Building General Flowchart

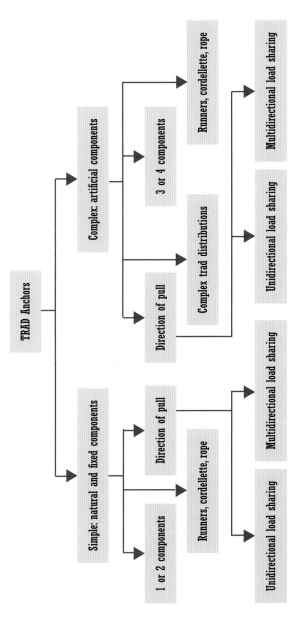

Anchor Building and System Forces

The following terms describe system forces in relation to anchor building. They should be taken into consideration when building an anchor on a trad climb.

Direction of pull: This is the direction the anchor will be pulled or loaded when a climber falls on it. Generally this will be toward the last protection component placed on the climb.

Elongation: All anchors will stretch when loaded. The amount of stretch depends on material type, material amount, material configuration: single strand or loop and if material is knotted or straight. Planning for this stretch is difficult. Ideally stretch results in a still functional master point—chest to eye level.

Equalized or equalizing: It is *very rare* for an anchor to be perfectly equalized, with each component piece taking exactly the same amount of force. This is a flawed anchor concept.

Load sharing: This is what effectively built anchors do—share the load from the forces applied to its protection components via the attachment rigging. Each

Simple Anchors

Natural Component Anchors with a Monolith

A common occurrence on trad climbs is for a natural component monolith, unquestionably secure and solid, to be utilized as an anchor. There are numerous ways to build these anchors and adhere to NERDSS principles. For example with a cordellette, there are a few options:

piece will receive some of the force applied if there is *intelligent load distribution*. Rigging specifics will determine how this force distribution occurs.

Multidirectional: Anchor is rigged with a method that will have multiple directions of pull (or a small range of directions) that best share/distribute the load.

Multidirectional anchors have the potential to extend and shock load. They usually have a range of direction of pull that will result in load sharing to all of the component protection. It is virtually impossible for this load sharing to result in equal force on each of the component protection pieces.

Off-axis loading: When using a unidirectional anchor rigging, a shift in the direction of pull will result in off-axis loading, which in turn could result in all the forces being applied to only one of the protection components. Not ideal.

Unidirectional: This means the anchor is rigged with a method that will have one direction of pull that best shares the loads. These anchors usually do not have much extension or shock load potential, and they typically do not load share equally between the components.

- Tree wrap (creates a "sticky" master point and vertical shelf)
- Doubled up (creates a master point and vertical shelf)

Trad anchor: tree wrap (modified wrap three, pull two) on a monolith.

Fixed Component Anchors

Another common occurrence on trad climbs is for a fixed anchor to be present. There are numerous ways to build these anchors and adhere to NERDSS principles. For example with a cordellette there are a few common options—Quad, pony tail.

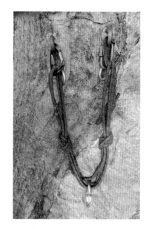

Trad anchors: Quad on two modern bolts.

Complex Anchors

When a leader resorts to building an anchor with three or more pieces of removable protection, anchoring gets more complicated, and those complications are compounded by the availability of resources and the needs of the anchor to be loaded in different directions. In each case, the anchor builder will need, at the least, anchoring tools, like a cordellette or a couple of 4-foot runners, to affect any sort of solution. Each of the techniques we propose requires those tools. So the question presents itself: What if the leader does not have those tools? It is never prudent or commendable to belay from an inadequate anchor. If the leader does not have appropriate tools or knowledge to build an anchor, retreat is probably the most appropriate option. Retreating still requires some anchoring or down-climbing and some strategies for this are discussed on pages 113–15.

Building Three- or Four-Piece Anchors

The cordellette is an amazingly versatile tool for combining three or four removable pieces. Most of the time, these kinds of anchors are satisfactory because the anchor builder has enough gear and the direction of load is unidirectional.

The pony tail anchor with artificial removable components.

Building with Limited/ Suboptimal Resources

The biggest challenge when building an anchor with limited or suboptimal resources is optimizing the holding power of the anchor. The variable placement locations or protection components available might not necessarily be one's first choice for anchor building. If the leader had not placed critical pieces during the lead, these kinds of complex strategies might not be needed. In other words, when faced with limited resources, anchor builders should learn to intentionally manipulate load distribution to make strong pieces hold more weight than weak pieces. Smartly rigging with more suboptimal pieces to the build can also help.

Building When the Direction of Load Will Be Variable

The self-adjusting systems we have seen in sport climbing and toproping are valuable tools in traditional lead climbing, too. The Quad is a versatile tool for the multidirectional load sharing to the components that is required.

Trad Quad Building: Steps 1, 2, and 3.

1. *Place protection.*

2. *Get cordellette and clip it though two pieces and pull through the middle all the way to the end of the cordellette loop; watch joining knot location.*

3. *Gather all strands and tie an overhand knot.*

4. *Extend down 10 to 15 inches, and gather all strands and tie another overhand knot.*

5. *Save the best component piece for last (it gets more force), and clip the free loops from the bottom of the rigging up into it. If you are building a trad Quad with four pieces, you may need to split these finishing loops and clove hitch one or both into components to ensure load sharing.*

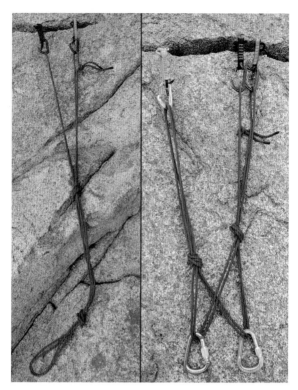

Trad Quad Building: Step 4 (L) and Step 5 (R).

Situations for the Trad Quad

- Multiple directions of pull or fall.
- Load share and stabilize components.
- Change of directions in multipitch—second comes to the belay from one direction, the next leader heads off in another.

Top to bottom: Pony tail, single strand pony tail, and trad Quad rigged on same components.

Anchor Building Specific Flowchart: Simple and Complex

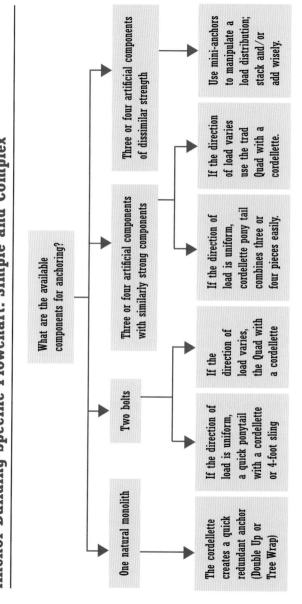

What are the available components for anchoring?

One natural monolith

The cordellette creates a quick redundant anchor (Double Up or Tree Wrap)

Two bolts

If the direction of load is uniform, a quick ponytail with a cordellette or 4-foot sling

If the direction of load varies, the Quad with a cordellette

Three or four artificial components with similarly strong components

If the direction of load is uniform, cordellette pony tail combines three or four pieces easily.

If the direction of load varies use the trad Quad with a cordellette.

Three or four artificial components of dissimilar strength

Use mini-anchors to manipulate a load distribution; stack and/or add wisely.

If we revisit the pitfalls to anchor strength and view them in the context of a trad anchor build, the pitfall of weak or faulty components clearly is the greatest source of errors. If the artificial protection components are all high, the anchor build follows logically and smoothly and can take many forms.

Pitfalls to Anchor Strength

- Weak or faulty components, poor component selection

- Weak or faulty attachment materials

- Catastrophic mistakes in master points, knot tying, carabiner usage

Anchor Building in the Lead Climbing Sequence

Upon arrival at the site you intend to belay, the order of events can either keep a leader safe while the anchor is being constructed, or expose the leader to a lead fall while the anchor is being constructed. Since the leader is interacting with components anyway, it seems wise to use those components as protection while the anchor is being built. Select a strong component and clip the rope to it with a quickdraw/runner or some other connection. Be careful not to use the carabiners that connect the anchoring material, or the climbing rope will be have to be removed from the anchor attachments.

The following steps outline the process:

1. Get safe—place your first component, evaluate it, clip a runner to it, and clip the climbing rope into the runner; the belay now functions through this component and manages risk. You created a mini toprope to protect your anchor rigging process.

2. Determine stance, protection options, material options, and direction of pull.

3. Determine building method.

   a. Unidirectional pony tail: one direction of pull, components are close together.

   b. Unidirectional single strand pony tail: one direction of pull, components are farther apart.

   c. Multidirectional trad Quad: multiple directions of pull possible, components are close together.

   d. Multidirectional trad Quad: multiple directions of pull possible, components are farther apart and may need additional attachment materials.

   e. Limited or suboptimal resources (multi- or unidirectional): stacked anchors, more components, mini anchors, deliberate manipulation of force distribution.

4. Build anchor.

5. Clip into master point (clove hitch with climbing rope or other method).

6. Declare "off belay" and begin organizing and preparing to use the anchor for a top belay, lower, rappel, and so on.

The question of knowing the number of components to utilize can be answered with an understanding of anchor principles and scoring individual

Even if there is a stance, manage risk immediately when arriving at an anchor—create a mini toprope to protect your anchor-rigging process.

components via RADSS. We can generalize these answers to some anchor baselines, which should simplify/inform a trad anchor build.

Artificial Anchor Baselines

Multipitch or top belay anchor (with belayer present) strive for a total component score of 9 or greater from protection analaysis via RADSS. This quantitative grading system "scores" an anchor:

- Belayer is present to continually evaluate and potentially correct errors.

- It can be located on top of a cliff or midcliff on multipitch routes.

Some Baseline Examples for Trad Anchors

See *Climbing: Protection* for more on RADSS scoring.

Components	Multipitch top/belay anchor
Natural monolith	One (12)
Threads or other natural components	Two (12, 2@6)
Modern bolts	Two (12, 2@6)
Pitons	Two (10, 2@5) Look to back up if only two present.
Artificial	Three (9+, 3@3+) At least three pieces of protection and each has a score of 3 or better. Never use an artificial component that is scored a 1.

Summary of Anchoring Tips and Considerations

- Are you at the established belay location?

- Be creative—look around. Evaluate and utilize acceptable components and attachments.

- Be conservative—the security of yourself and others depends on it.

- Spread out your components if possible. This can add stability and doesn't put all your eggs in one bad rock basket. One good rock basket is OK.

- The bigger and stronger the component pieces, the better.

- The direction of pull for the components should be toward the master point, which should be in alignment with the direction of pull from falls or lowers.

- There should never be a piece of artificial protection with a RADSS score of 0 or 1 in any anchor.

- Consider stance, belay station organization, and desired load sharing.

- Be efficient—time is for climbing.

Why Are There So Many Ways to Anchor?

There are even more methods out there. We have tried to streamline the anchoring process. Having an understanding of the riggings above gives a builder choice and a skill set to build with multiple attachment materials. The materials at hand should not matter; a NERDSS anchor can be built regardless, and a forgotten attachment material should not cause a spike in risk. It is important to know multiple methods for each type of anchor using multiple materials. You will then be able to deal with numerous expected and unexpected situations to build a good anchor. Having multiple tools in your anchor toolbox will serve you well.

Connecting to the Anchor

Connecting yourself to an anchor at the top of a cliff should be a skill familiar from cleaning and rappelling applications used in sport climbing. It is also a valuable trad skill for the same applications but is also used in order to soundly belay or transition the rope.

Ways to Connect to an Anchor at the Top of a Trad Climb

- Use a nylon sling or daisy link (Personal Anchoring System, PAS).

  - Girth hitch to hard points of the harness, also known as the soft good path. This path mirrors that of the belay loop. Avoid girth hitching to the belay loop.

  - Clip it to the anchor's master point with a locking carabiner.

- Use a single strand of climbing rope.

  - Clove hitch above your tie-in knot and clip to the anchor's master point with a locking carabiner. Adjust as necessary.

Notes

- All the methods utilized on fixed anchors in sport climbing applications could also be applied to fixed anchors in trad climbing. However, they may not all be practical.

- Double-check your connections to anchors (correct location in the master point, correct attachment to harness, and carabiner locked) and stay underneath, tight and secure on whatever connection you use.

CHAPTER 8

Movement and Managing the Rope

Toproping outdoors prepares a traditional lead climber to interpret lines of weakness that one would never encounter at an indoor climbing gym. Cracks, slabs, corners, and dihedrals can be learned and anticipated via toproping or on a variety of boulder problems. Furthermore, sport climbing prepares a leader to travel with a rope trailing behind her legs. Projecting sport climbs teaches a leader to take lead falls. So, in many ways, the aspiring trad leader already has a strong foundation for movement skills like jamming, stemming, smearing, drop knees, and dynos, as well as leading skills like managing the rope, clipping, and anchoring.

This focus of this text is not to discuss or present these movement techniques or technical movement skills; see our other books for that. This not a climbing technique, toproping, or sport climbing text, but these skills are very much relevant to trad climbing and briefly described in terms of crack climbing. This type of movement is often most identified with trad climbing, but not all trad climbing involves crack climbing. It is important to review this movement because it will be necessary to create stances, place protection, and manage risk. When crack climbing, you are putting some part of your body (or your whole body) in a crack and figuring out a way to make it stay in place through wedging or by making it bigger, creating oppositional forces allowing the part to stay in the crack and aid your climbing—jamming.

Many cracks are climbed using the opposition techniques common to other climbing disciplines. The straight-in form of crack climbing has two main variations in its techniques:

1. **Constriction jam:** Target a constriction in the crack and simply wedge the appropriate-size body part into the crack.

2. **Compression jam:** Target a parallel crack and a body part is torqued, twisted, fattened, or squeezed to apply outward pressure to the two parallel surfaces.

Trad Climbing Tips—Cracks

- Look for constrictions to jam, and be prepared to use compression jams in parallel cracks.

- Be creative. Look outside the crack for holds.

- Take rests only when absolutely needed—keep moving.

- Commit to movement and efficiency.

- Be creative!

- Consider hand taping. This will protect hands and make stances more comfortable and potentially secure.

Unlike toproping and sport climbing, the traditional lead climber must learn to lead with more equipment, which translates into a heavier and more strenuous lead climb. The traditional lead climber must learn sustainable stances to place protection, or she must learn to place protection so efficiently and at the appropriate times that she can move forward without huge penalties in overall endurance. Lastly, a trad leader will discover quickly that a row of bolts will not dictate the line the rope travels; his placements and extensions will. As a result, the trad leader must be able to envision the entire pitch, see his entire rope line, and keep it as straight as possible by positioning placements and extensions via quickdraws, runners, or extendable runners appropriately. These attachments can also in some cases increase protection stability as well as keep the rope running straight. In this chapter, we will explore how the rack, the rope, and the inexact position of protection affect a lead climber's movement.

Leading and Falling with a Rack

A massive rack of equipment means that a climber's overall mass is greater. As a result, each move is slightly more strenuous, but overall the entire lead is more exhausting when leading in a traditional style. Lead climbers can do careful research and be certain to carry only a precise amount of protection, but many climbs cannot be perfectly forecasted. Often, traditional lead climbers carry more equipment than they actually need to account for this kind of uncertainty. Accordingly, more conditioning, more training, and more overall toughness might be required to lead trad climbs.

Similarly, taking a fall with tons of extra equipment can be a loud and clattering experience. Lead climbers are well advised to approach trad leads with ample experience falling, and there are few ways better than sport climbing to learn. An experienced and skilled sport leader will have instincts to fall with limbs bent, ready to absorb impact. She will have an instinct to right herself and fall upright.

Those skills and instincts are absolutely vital to the traditional lead climber because traditional leads ask the leader to contend with dangerous falls. Ledges, runouts, and body-swallowing features do not always allow the leader to take nice clean falls. Leaders will have to learn to skate down runout slabs. They will have to learn to slip out of inverted double foot jams on overhanging off-width crags, right themselves, and fall upright. They will have to learn to protect and clip past ledges that might break legs and ankles.

Falling Tips

- Have a good belayer.

- Be aware of hazards in landing area.

- Communicate—use commands such as "watch me" and "falling."

- Become a falling cat: Relax, breathe, and become a shock absorber.

- Bend legs and arms, with hands out.

- Don't push off.

- Legs should hit the rock first.

Falling Practice

With a desire to get better at falling, a knowledge of how to fall, a knowledge of falling hazards and some basic physics, falling practice can be set up and managed. Like any skill, you will get better at falling if you practice. Practice and the resulting skill building can also alleviate fears when climbing. Set yourself up for success when practicing. Choose terrain that is slightly overhanging and somewhat long. Sport climbs with modern protection bolts are best for this. The practice should occur far up the climb, where there is substantial rope in the system to utilize the dynamic properties of a climber's most important tool—the rope. Start at this high point of the climb, falling on a "mini toprope." Fall under the clipped fixed protection. Now move to be even with the quickdraw and fall. Repeat and gradually move up, leaving the security of the mini toprope and proximity to the quickdraw and start taking small lead falls, 1 foot above quickdraw, 2 feet above quickdraws, and so on. Progress with good falling technique and ensure you constantly assess the hazards as the terrain and fall paths change. Some will use a locked locker draw to enhance security for this falling practice.

If confidence in artificial protection is a skill still to be developed, consider practicing managed falls on trad gear. Working with the same principles outlined above, place a few solid components close together. Attach runners where appropriate. This will back up the top piece of protection to be fallen upon. When in doubt about protection quality, have an experienced trad climber place this protection or integrate two pieces of protection for this practice. Practice, increasing fall distances as desired, and be careful!

There are many cases where a fall is not ideal. This is the case when a climber cannot become a shock absorber and will hit something hard. Low angle rock, landing zones with ledges, blocks, flakes, and belayers are all hard; hitting them will be unpleasant. You can avoid routes of this nature or ensure they are well within your abilities. You should be aware of the route's characteristics and make informed decisions. If the rope is not clear and behind a leg, a fall could yield rope burns at a minimum, or complete inversion and head-first fall (along with the rope burns) a strong possibility. A rope that is clear is one that is in front of the climber's body and positioned with the direction of movement in mind. If this direction is straight up, the rope should be in front of the body and straight up between the legs. If the climbing direction is to the left, the rope should be in front and coming off the right hip. If the climbing direction is to the right, the rope should be in front and coming off the left hip. Falling when a clipping error has occurred is another hazard to avoid.

Clear the rope. This climber could experience rope burns and likely flip over if a fall were to occur.

Prioritize the Stance

Placing protection and clipping is more time-consuming than clipping bolts, even for the best trad climbers in the world. So, traditional lead climbers must have a strong instinct for finding a stance to place protection. Leaders need to be efficient, or they will simply bumble around, run out of energy, and not manage risk as effectively.

The "Five Gets" can help keep a trad climber moving:

1. Get a stable stance.

2. Get a protection component placed.

3. Determine the need for extension. Get an attachment connected to the component, adding or extending a runner when necessary.

4. Get the climbing rope clipped into the attachment.

5. Get moving.

Clipping

Clipping the rope into a protection component or clipping a runner into a protection component and then the rope into it seems simple, and yet a complex negotiation of some very specific risks must also happen in those steps. We commonly witness a high volume of errors around the skills of clipping. While Z-clipping the rope is less common in trad climbing, it can still occur. Back clipping, missed clips/dropped rope when clipping, or inefficient technique happen all the time during the vital process of clipping when trad climbing.

What if you back clip? Stop your advance up the climb and return to the scene of the error. Leave the back-clipped runner in place, and attempt to leapfrog in a new and correct one. Once a properly clipped runner is in place, you can clean the original incorrect one.

What if you Z-clip? Stop your advance up the climb and return to the scene of the error. Unclip the rope from the last runner and reclip it in the correct manner. The belayer is a watchful eye and risk manager for the climber and could help prevent these errors.

The clipping process ideally occurs at about waist to chest height—not too high and not too low. Sometimes a protection component is placed higher up from a good stance and is then clipped. Be aware if the leader reaches up to clip, slack must be pulled into the belay to reach up to that clip. If an unexpected fall happens at that moment, the extra distance will be added to the length of the lead fall. An awareness of these consequences is important. However, a leader should not hesitate to reach up to clip if that stance increases the likelihood of actually making the clip. Long fall potential and bad (awkward/strenuous) stances are not a good combo to clip from.

Clipping Commands

Leader: **"Clipping."** Leader is ready to clip the rope. Belayer needs to give an appropriate amount of slack.

Belayer: Gives approximately two to three arm lengths of slack.

Leader: **"Clipped."** Leader has clipped rope into runner/quickdraw.

Belayer: Belays excessive slack out of the system.

Rope Clipping

CLIPPING THE ROPE

1. Start with your hand at your tie-in knot.

2. Move your hand down the rope.

3. Communicate clipping.

4. Pull up the rope.

5. Use a comfortable method to clip the rope into the carabiner.

6. Communicate clipped.

7. Examine for errors.

8. Climb on.

There are numerous hand techniques to facilitate clipping the rope. Two common ones are outlined below. Many climbers use different techniques depending on which way the carabiner faces, which side of the body the carabiner is located on, and which hand is free to clip.

1. **Finger method.** Grab the rope between thumb and a finger(s) and stabilize the carabiner with a different finger while clipping the rope into the carabiner. The finger method usually involves stabilizing the carabiner with your middle finger and clipping the rope while it is held/pushed by the thumb and index finger. The middle finger serves as a stabilizing pivot point for clipping.

2. **Big pinch method.** Grab the rope between thumb and a finger or rest it in the notch between thumb and fingers. Pinch the whole carabiner while clipping the rope into the carabiner. The big pinch method commonly involves pinching the carabiner with the whole hand. The rope is

Clipping methods: left side (top and bottom)—big pinches; right side (top and bottom)—finger methods.

clipped from a resting point at the base of the thumb or from between two fingers.

There are eight possible clipping positions based on the three clipping variables: Clipping hand, side of body clip is on, and in direction the gate faces. (See *Climbing: From Toproping to Sport* in the How to Climb series for complete list.) These orientations should be practiced!

Managing the Rope's Line

Unlike sport climbing, the trad leader can place protection where he chooses, often as frequently as he chooses. The leader should have a thought process and be guided by the following:

Protection Thought Process Expanded

- Is there a need? Why?

- Location: Where and when can I meet that need?

- Application: What can I use to meet that need, and how (utilization of component and attachment process)?

- Create a manageable protection frequency— protect the climb.

- Protect runouts—which seems like an oxymoron as a runout is a section of a climb with no protection. Awareness of these sections will allow you to protect immediately before and after a runout to manage risk. Don't unnecessarily create runouts by choosing to not utilize protection opportunities present.

- Protect cruxes (very difficult sections or moves).

- Protect ledges; minimize the potential of falling on a ledge. Some may need another omnidirectional.

- Protect the second (i.e., traverses) and set them up for success with easy cleaning.

- Protect the rope: Divert and keep the rope away from a feature where it may become stuck or run over a sharp feature. Do not let it get entangled in your legs or with your body.

- Protect the pathway—keep the rope running as straight as possible. Angular, zigzagging rope paths will cause rope drag, which can hinder a leader's progress and make climbing much less enjoyable. Using runners and possibly extending them can help protect the pathway.

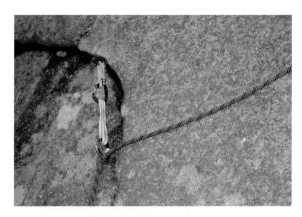

This protection rope clip in point has been extended with a runner. Extend it further by expanding the runner to its full length; this would lessen the bend in the rope and provide a straighter situation with less friction-producing drag that can weigh down a climber.

The front portrait of the rope line is straight.

The front portrait of the rope line is not straight—rope drag here we come.

At all times, the leader must be able to conjure a mental picture of the pitch he is leading. He should be able to see the side and front profiles of his rope line: Both should run in a straight line (as straight as possible) from the belayer to the climber.

Managing Risk with Movement

Many traditional lead climbs pose hazards and risks to the lead climber that cannot be solved by placing protection, by an attentive belayer, or any sort of technical trickery. Climbs with an "R" or an "X" rating, for example, have sections of climber where lead falls will predictably result in long falls, perhaps injury or even, perhaps death. Risks and runouts of that magnitude can only be managed by climbing flawlessly, and by not falling. For many climbs, the dangerous sections of the lead happen when the climbing is not as difficult or as strenuous as other sections. So, a fall is perhaps less likely. But, long falls are no less consequential on easy terrain than they are on hard terrain. In many cases, long falls on easy terrain are more significant because the terrain has protruding features and ledges.

When the only way to manage the risks of a long fall is to climb flawlessly, a prudent leader climb will inspect hold and footing more carefully, move more cautiously, and put the belayer on notice regarding the severity of the terrain ahead. If nothing else, a lead climber should be able to see these risks coming when they research a climb or perform visual mapping before the lead. Often, however, the protection you anticipate is not available, the equipment is not available, or the rock face has changed from its original state. Either way, the leader will discover a runout section of climbing while they are leading. Too often, the disheartened leader chooses to push forward, increasing the severity of the risk. The leader should always consider down-climbing and retreating as a viable option. No adventure is worth severe injury or death.

Practice Down-Climbing

Toproping and sport climbing do not necessarily teach a climber the crucial skill of down-climbing. Down-climbing is one of the most valuable retreat skills, and it allows a leader to reverse an errant course without leaving gear behind. It is important to appreciate that the risks involved in down-climbing are exactly the same as those entertained on the way up. If fall consequences were acceptable on the way up, they should also be acceptable on the way down. Yet many leaders do not perceive this to be the case because they have not practiced down-climbing. They perceive a higher fall probability with the unfamiliar style of movement. So make it more familiar. Climbing gyms and toprope settings make it easy for a climber to practice down-climbing. On your next gym or toproping session, try down-climbing every pitch as well as up-climbing it.

Retreating

At some point the leader may have had enough and will look to return to earth. Down-climbing is an option. Aid climbing up to the anchor is an option. In trad settings this becomes a more complex endeavor requiring a large volume of equipment. If you have this skill set and equipment and use it to get to an anchor, it can be used to lower off and clean your protection via processes outlined in this text.

If aid climbing is not an option or desirable, a more immediate lower from the climb is required. The best practice of redundancy should be adhered to. This means using/leaving at least two protection components to lower off from. Even better is to create an anchor and use it to belay your second, who may be able to further the team's progress or use the anchor to engage in lowering process. Someone else may be able to retrieve them for you or if "lost," they are a small price to pay for your safety and are easily replaceable. You are worth it!

Seconding the Climb

There is also important movement by the second, although a bit different in nature as it is protected by the leader's top belay—a toprope. Seconds need to be efficient in their movement and clean the leader's protection. They manage risk through efficiency, and keep the rack organized as they remove protection. Cleaning adds another task and difficulty to the climb, and if it is fumbly, it can make the climbing less enjoyable, more strenuous, and the loss of equipment a possibility. Hopefully the following sequence helps manage these challenges:

1. As soon as the second is on belay, he cleans his anchor and begins climbing.

2. As protection is reached, first remove the piece while it is still clipped to the rope.

3. Clip the carabiner on the protection piece to the harness or gear sling. (If the runner is extended, it may be easier to sling it over your shoulder, unclip the protection piece from it, and rebuild runners

A second cleaning.

at the belay station. You need a good stance and steady hands to rebuild a runner while seconding.)

4. Finally, unclip the runner from the rope. This system guards against dropping gear.

5. Repeat as necessary for the duration of the climb.

Cleaning Tips

Practice cleaning gear on the ground; this will let you see the whole picture, in and out, and give you lots of repetition.

- Go lightly when using a nut tool and try to reverse the path the component was placed in.

- This is an art form. It is easy to make some placements even harder to remove if they are pushed or pulled in the wrong direction—be careful!

- Some new to cleaning will tether their nut tool so they don't drop it. This can have a huge consequence if it is necessary to remove important protection to use later.

CHAPTER 9

Rappelling

Hopefully the reader has an understanding of rappelling. Knowing the best practices, different types of rappels, and various belay and rappel devices is helpful and necessary prior to engaging in this skill. Rappelling is a high-risk pursuit within the high-risk pursuit of trad climbing. The rappelling risks increase further when two ropes are joined or when multiple rappels (with the associated anchor transitions) are necessary to return to earth. In many instances, there will be no partner to exchange communication and checks with; these cues and extra risk-management eyes will simply not be present.

Backed-up extended autoblock rappel.

Rappelling Best Practices

- Use a backup.

- Manage the rope: Are both ends going where you want them?

- Close system—tie knots in both ends of your rope.

Rappelling and Trad Climbing

Rappelling is an essential tool for traditional lead climbing for several reasons. First, single pitch climbs (less than half the rope length) often involve rappelling in the cleaning sequence. Unlike sport climbs, there is no guarantee that the permanent anchors on a trad climb will be conducive to lowering, so rappelling is often the most practical way to descend while cleaning. Second, longer rappels will involve tying two ropes together and descending from a rappel station that might be used on every route in the sector. In the one case, the cleaner will need to rappel. In the second, the leader and the second may need to rappel.

Cleaning a Single Pitch Route by Rappelling

If the second or the leader wishes to clean a route by rappelling, the sequence of events could either produce a smooth and efficient process or it could result in mishap, as an unfortunate number of accidents do. The biggest difference between cleaning by rappelling and cleaning by lowering is that the cleaner must relinquish one safety system (the belay), establish a second system (a tether), and finally transition to a third system (the rappel). These transitions provide opportunities for oversight and error, so practice, attentiveness, and double checks are crucial. The reader should understand and intuit that the rappelling cleaning sequence puts the cleaner in a position all alone, at the anchor, with no belay system as a backup. The plan to rappel should be clearly communicated to the belayer before the climb or cleaning begins.

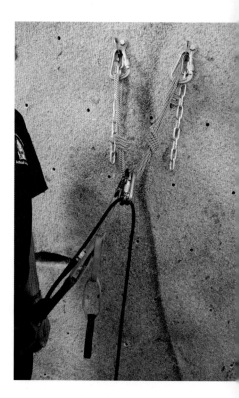

Step 1: Connect. Upon arriving at the anchor, connect to its master point via an acceptable method, and work without maintaining a stance or a grip on the rock. Double-check to make sure the connection is secure and the carabiner is locked.

Step 2: Call "Off belay." Communicate with the belayer and await a response.

Step 3: Secure the rope.
Once tethered to the master point and double-checked, call "Slack." Pull up slack to tie a figure 8 on a bight and connect the bight knot to the belay loop with a locking carabiner. The rope cannot be dropped with this sequence!

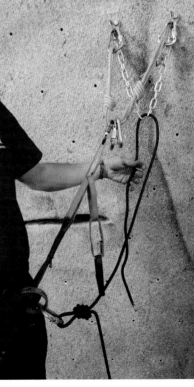

Step 4a and b: Untie the original figure 8 follow through, pass through anchor, and tie a stopper knot. Thread the tail through the rap rings or chain links, and tie a bulky stopper knot. The overhand on a bight is a good one. This knot will stop the rope from falling back through the rings and will close one end of the system, so be sure that it is bulky and tight.

Step 5: Detach and untie the figure 8 on a bight. Detach and untie the rope securing figure 8 on a bight that was connected to the belay loop.

Step 6: Pull the rope through the rings. Pull until the middle of the rope is at the anchor and both ends of the rope are on the ground with system-closing knots in each end.

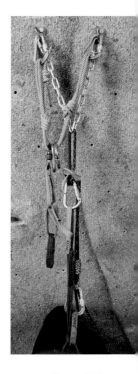

Step 7: Rig for rappel. Using an MBD (plate/aperture/tube device), set up both strands of rope in adjacent slots on the belay device. Connect and extend the belay device with a locking carabiner to the personal tether.

Step 8: Tie a friction hitch backup. Tie a backup, like an autoblock, around the two brake strands, and connect the hitch to the belay loop with a locking carabiner.

Step 9: Double-check all critical links. Make sure carabiners are locked, rappel is rigged correctly, middle of rope passes through rappel rings, and rope ends are on the ground with system-closing knots in each end.

Step 10: Detach personal tether from the anchor. Clean anchor. Rappel.

The reader should understand and intuit that the rappelling cleaning sequence puts the cleaner in a position all alone, at the anchor, with no belay system as a backup. So, it is a sequence that is replete with opportunities for error. It is a sequence that should be practiced on the ground and thoroughly understood before being undertaken. Most of all, it is a technique whose clear applications are so rare, it is probably best reserved for those occasions where it is absolutely necessary. Sport climbers will hopefully applaud the day when it is finally extinct from the discipline.

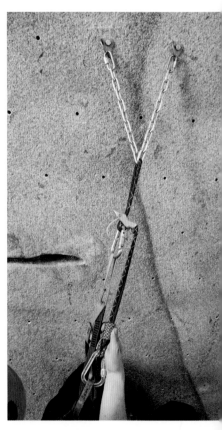

A backed-up carabiner break—an option if you drop a rappel device!

Rappelling with an ABD

When a blocking knot is added to a rappel, it essentially fixes one side of the rope while leaving the other free to be pulled from below. As a result, there is an

ABD Rappelling Tips

- Use the ABD as if you are lowering a climber. When rappelling with an ABD, you are lowering yourself.

- Be gentle with the lever.

- Keep a brake hand on at all times.

- If you desire or need to go hands-free, you can tie a catastrophe knot (e.g., overhand on a bight) in the brake strand close to the device.

opportunity to rappel the single strand with an assisted braking device, like a GriGri. Many trad climbers who are fond of the GriGri routinely adopt this rappelling technique, while others use the counterweight

Rappelling with an ABD. The BHK and carabiner block the rappelling strand against the rap rings. The opposite strand can be retrieved by pulling down, so rappelling on the correct strand is vital.

Counterweight rappel.

rappel—both require the rappel to be less than half the rope length. Double-check that your rope will work for these applications and follow rappelling best practices.

Rappelling with Two Ropes

The other most common practice for rappelling in trad climbing involves the use of a second rope to make a longer rappel. In this scenario, the second climber typically trails a second rope or carries it in a backpack. It is important to appreciate that the climbing team is dealing with a series or transition sequences that happen while both members are high off the ground, in high-stakes terrain. The Big Plan conversation should be held and resolved before the critical transitions take place. In sequence, the second climber should be carrying the second rope, belayed from the top by the leader. The transitions begin immediately when the second arrives at the anchor.

1. **The second anchors with a tether** to the master point with a locking carabiner. Once he's done, he quickly double-checks his connection before announcing "off belay" to the leader.

2. **Pull the rope through the rings and attach the ropes together.** The second can now untie the belay rope, thread it through the rap rings, and tie the rope to the end of the second rope end he has either trailed or carried (flat overhand). If necessary, the second rope can be secured before it is detached from the climber.

3. **Rig both climbers for rappel with extensions.** Both climbers rig for rappel on both strands of rope. One will have to be rigged in front of the other, and the first rappeller should also rig a friction hitch backup, like an autoblock.

The flat overhand for joining rappel ropes. It should be dressed, stressed, and have 1-foot tails. It is efficient to tie and untie, has a low profile to minimize the chances of getting stuck, and has a long history of successful use. Remember which side to pull to retrieve it.

Avoid getting ropes stuck by following these instructions:

- Use a low-profile joining knot, like the flat overhand.

- Set up and pull the side that will best help prevent jams. Pull away from constrictions and entrapments.

- Untie knots and untangle all ropes before pulling.

- In windy conditions, avoid trailing or tossing. Carry the second rope in a backpack while climbing and holster it (with butterfly coils gathered and held at the middle by a sling, then clipped to harness) while rappelling.

4. **Double checks.** Both climbers should double-check each other's attachment carabiners and rappel setups, and the first rappel should double-check the backup. Once all double checks are complete, the anchor and the connections to it can be disassembled and cleaned.

5. **Manage ropes.** At this point, if the second has trailed a rope, one end of the second rope should be tied to the other end of the original lead rope; the other end of the second rope should still be on the ground. The other end of the lead should still be tied to the leader. Now the rappelling system is effectively closed. The first rappeller can either lower or holster the coils of rope that remain at the belay. There is no need to toss them onto unsuspecting people below.

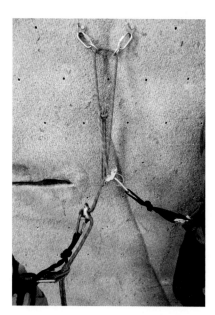

Climbers ready to rappel with two ropes. Note the autoblock friction hitch backup for the first rappeller.

6. **The first climber rappels** to ground, managing the backup as she does so. Once she arrives on the ground, she calls "off rappel" to the second climber and gives that climber a backup with a fireman's belay. The first climber can leave the back up friction hitch (autoblock) on the rope to enhance the fireman belay's security.

The second rappeller is given a fireman's belay as a backup. If a fireman's belay is unavailable for the second rappeller, a friction hitch backup should be used.

7. **Pull the ropes** to the ground and steer clear of the tumbling rope end. It is customary to call out "rope!" when this rope end hurtles toward the ground. Make sure your system closing knots were untied so as to knot jam the rope into the anchor above.

Other Notes on Rappelling

There are many discrete variations to the techniques mentioned in this chapter: transitions from top belay to rappelling with only one rope, lowering the second instead of having him rappel, simul-rappelling both climbers on single strands with ABDs (they counterbalance each other). There are many efficiencies and variations to discover that are beyond the scope of this text. Guidance from an AMGA-certified instructor or guide can be a great way to expand upon the concepts illustrated in this chapter.

Emergency Preparedness, Assistance, and Improvised Rescue

B ecause the essential allure of traditional lead climbing involves managing risk, it is more than conceivable that each climbing team's learning curve might one day involve an injury or an accident. If nothing else, experienced trad climbers are likely sometime to interact with other parties in crisis. What is the trad climber to do? Be prepared and organized, and practice certain skills regularly. The ability to self-rescue is essential given the complex and sometimes remote nature of trad climbs. The possible emergency situations are too voluminous to cover fully, but the solutions all involve a few key skills that can be learned, rehearsed, and reinforced by mentors and professional instructors. This chapter briefly explores first aid preparedness, what to do when the leader is in trouble, what to do when the belayer is in trouble, and what to do when the second is in trouble. There is more information on these topics in our other works in this series.

First Aid Training and Supplies

At a minimum, all outdoor rock climbers should take a basic first aid and cardiopulmonary resuscitation

(CPR) class. For these reasons, many climbers and most professional climbing instructors and guides maintain a Wilderness First Responder level of first aid training and a professional rescuer level of CPR. Whatever level of training an individual has achieved should be complemented with a corresponding first aid kit. Its contents should be in good condition, organized, and not expired. There are numerous sources to determine the contents. Your supplies should be researched and specific to the climbing site.

Logistical Organization

Prior planning and organization are a big part of trad climbing. In addition to the climb and climbing area and equipment specifics, the following logistical preparations should be a part of every outing:

- Leave plans with a family member or friend.
- Plan approaches and retreats. Carry maps, guidebooks, and other information on these areas.
- Have emergency numbers and hospital directions, and know where to find the nearest help or reliable phone service.
- Be aware of local hazards: bugs, poisonous plants, animals, and other environmental concerns.
- Make the Big Plan for the climb.

Communication

Outdoor climbers must be prepared to call for help. Here are some considerations for communication:

- Will I have to move to get reliable cell phone coverage?

- Will I need a spare battery or a way to recharge?

- Will I need a satellite telephone, communicators, and/or radios?

- What are the professionals using?

- Has the selected system been tested in the specific terrain/location?

Technical Best Practices

Awareness of common risky "spidey sense" moments like managing runouts, marginal protection, anchoring, clipping, lowering, and rappelling is necessary. The procedures and best practices for these skills have been outlined in this text. Here are some technical best practices from these skills that transfer to emergency procedures:

- Tie relevant backup knots and make relevant connections for yourself and any person in need.

- Back up rappels and lowers.

- Don't get in a "PICL": **P**rusik (or other friction hitch) **I**s **C**ritical **L**ink.

How to Help a Belayer

When a belayer is injured or incapacitated, the responder is probably caring for two people simultaneously: the belayer and the climber they were belaying before the incident. The responder must take over the "bad" belay from the belayer to help both.

The responder should enter the system by taking control of the belayer's brake strand, setting up his own ABD (assuming he has one), and tying a backup knot.

With the new belay system attached to the responder, the injured belayer can be removed from the system. The climber can be directed to take his or her weight off the climbing rope so the belayer's device can be removed. The responder can then lower the climber to the ground and proceed to care for the belayer. This

Set up an independent belay system with an ABD on an injured belayer's brake strand.

procedure is also possible when the climber's end of the rope is weighted/unable to be unweighted. A friction hitch placed above the original belayer's device and connected to the responder's harness can serve as bridge and transfer system forces off the original belay and onto the responder, allowing the belay device to be freed as described.

How to Help a Leader

Most of the time, helping a leader is easy. They just need to be lowered to the ground. But in trad climbing especially, it is conceivable that an injured leader will arrest on a ledge or become badly stuck somehow, or that the injury will occur after more than half the rope has been introduced in the belay system. In these cases, lowering is not an option. Ascending on a counterweight can be a way to climb up to an injured leader using an ABD. Once there, the leader's injuries can be stabilized, the belayer and the leader can descend together; an anchor may need to be built to add security to this process. Because of the engagement of its camming mechanism, the ABD can be used as a progress capture for rope ascension. A Prusik and a double-length sling can be used as an ascender and an etrier (step). Together, the three tools will always allow rescuers to ascend a climbing rope. Here is the process for ascending with an ABD:

1. Slide a friction hitch runner combo up the rope and stand on it (the stand).

2. Pull rope through the ABD and sit on it (the sit).

3. Repeat the stand and sit maneuvers for continued upward progress.

4. Tie backup knots in the brake strand (overhand on a bight) every 10 feet or so.

Once the responder has accessed the injured leader, it will be difficult to descend as a climbing team, especially if the leader is injured. To provide an assisted lower, connect a 4-foot sling from the responder's harness (girth hitch) to the injured leader's belay loop (locking carabiner). Now, as the responder

Ascending with an ABD.

lowers, both leader and responder will lower simultaneously. If it is desired to more precisely position the injured person, the friction hitch used for ascending can be repositioned on the leader's rope strand. This can be connected to the responder's belay loop via the sling and a locking carabiner. Adjusting this friction hitch will position the injured leader as desired.

To descend with an ABD after ascending:

1. Tie a new backup.

2. Remove the friction hitch and runner and rappel with ABD.

3. Maintain a presence on the brake strand and untie the backup knots as you move down.

If the leader has climbed more than half the rope length into the belay system, things are a little bit more complicated for the responder. Rope ascension will allow the belayer to access the leader, but if the belayer tries to provider an assisted lower, there will not be enough rope to lower the leader all the way to ground. Instead, the belayer will have to be satisfied to lower the leader to the ground, and then ascend/aid the pitch to the point where the rope can be anchored to cams, bolts, or natural features. Now the belayer can rappel the fixed line to get to the ground.

Simple Aid Climbing

Aid climbing in its essence uses equipment to aid an ascent. There are many forms and expressions of this climbing style. Most are beyond the scope of this text. French Free or "frenching" is probably the most appropriate. This technique, named after French sport climbers, does not involve using a complex aid-climbing rigging. You merely pull on protection

Helping a Leader Summary

Go to baseline and set up ABD ascending rigging.

1. Counterweight ascend to stuck leader.

2. Reach leader, update your back-up knot. (You may need to build a bomb-proof anchor and put rope through it—take leader's gear for the build or other uses.) Take all their gear and construct a bombproof anchor.

3. Connect the victim to your harness with a back-up runner 1 girth hitch to your harness, 1 locking carabiner clip to the leader's belay loop.

4. Help the leader (care, unstick, etc.).

5. Breakdown ascend and build rappel.

   a. Undo friction hitch "sit" from ascend and switch it to the rope above the stuck climber and connect it to your belay loop with a locking carabiner. This will help equalize the counterweight rappel and help position the leader/keep them close.

6. Counterweight rappel with leader.

   a. Undo last backup knot.

   b. Rappel with ABD.

   c. Undo backup knots.

   d. Protect victim with your feet.

placements as you "climb," perhaps connecting an occasional sling to a protection placement to stand on or connecting your harness to a piece for planning/resting. This technique, as well as using full-blown aid-climbing rigs, can be a valuable tool.

How to Help a Second

Seconds can suffer a variety challenges, and most of the time the simplest thing to do is lower them to the ground. In the worst cases, the second may be carrying the second rope, and the leader will have to resort to fixing (securely connect to an anchor) the lead rope in order to descend and retrieve it. In other cases, however, it might be expeditious to raise the second. Sometimes, the second has merely fallen off of a steep section, and some assistance from above will help them regain their climbing holds in order to continue up the pitch. Hauls are ways to create a mechanical advantage to raise a fallen climber. To set up a haul, the belay must establish a hands-free workspace to build a hauling system. Many responders call this hands-free workspace "baseline."

Baseline

Baseline can have three main forms, but all do the same thing. They get you to a position of "strength" and "comfort"—the workspace to be hands free and gather yourself/equipment and plan to act. It is the "high ground" in a complex situation from which you can act. There are four broad categories of action that can be taken out of a baseline position: haul, ascend or leave when possible, rappel, and lower.

- **ABD baseline**—an ABD on an anchor with a secure catastrophe knot in the brake strand.

- **Plaquette baseline**—a belay device in plaquette mode on an anchor with a secure catastrophe knot in the brake strand.

- **Baseline**—the "original": a Munter mule overhand (MMO) on an anchor.

    Each of these baselines is pictured in this book.

Hauling Principles

Climbers for a variety of reasons may need to be hauled. They cannot finish the climb under their own power and they cannot be lowered to the ground. When you need to haul, get to baseline and set up a haul of choice. Understanding how hauling works is important. For example, a 3:1 haul will increase your pull power by a factor of 3. If you can pull with a force of 50 pounds, the 3:1 will increase this force to 150 pounds. However, it will take 3 feet hauling to raise a victim 1 foot. Every haul system will have a few consistent parts and variations on those parts. Every haul system will have a low-friction pulley point, a progress capture, and a puller (aka tractor). The most basic haul system consists entirely of those parts. It is possible to improvise a low-friction pulley and a progress capture using carabiners and friction hitches. But these systems are beyond the scope of this text. Suffice it to say that if hauls are a remote possibility, use an ABD or a plaquette to belay.

ABD or Plaquette 3:1 (Z-drag) Haul

1. From the ABD or plaquette baseline, place a friction hitch on the rope going to the climber (the puller/tractor).

2. Run the brake strand rope down through a carabiner attach it to the puller/tractor.

3. Pull. In this case, the ABD or plaquette is both a "low-friction" pulley and the progress capture. It provides a smooth point for the loaded rope to glide through, and captures the progress of the rope by only allowing the rope to move in one direction.

4. When the tractor approaches the ABD, the progress capture will hold the rope in place, and the belayer can slide the tractor back down to begin the cycle anew.

Drop a Loop 3:1 (essentially a 3:1 with no puller/tractor) Haul

1. From a 3:1 haul, apply a quick catastrophe knot to establish the baseline. Deconstruct the tractor and

Belay loop of person being hauled. They should also pull the middle strand of rope if possible.

A 3:1 haul with an ABD and a Drop a Loop 3:1 haul with a plaquette. The ABD and the plaquette can be applied to either of these hauls.

drop a loop of rope to the climber (this is possible only if he is less than one-third rope length away).

2. The climber clips the rope loop into his belay loop (locked locking carabiner is ideal here).

3. The climber pulls down on the middle belay/ brake strand of the rope, while the belayer pulls up on the redirected strand (climber should avoid pinching hand in carabiner when pulling).

Improvised Chest Harness

A simple but important tool for emergency procedures is an improvised chest harness. It can help support an injured climber in many ways. Constructed with a double-length sling: Pass one arm through the sling, wrap the sling under the other arm, and then tie around the starting point. The chest harness creates an attachment point that can keep the climber upright. This is a supportive connection to the system only— not for life safety.

Improvised chest harness.

Some Words on Technical Procedures

Before technical procedures are implemented a question has to be asked. Is there an easier, simpler way? Use soft skills where possible. Prevention is the biggest soft skill. Preparation and planning are the biggest parts of prevention. If prevention fails, communication and simple collaboration would be the softs skills to start with in a situation. The next question to ask is can gravity help the climbing team get safe? Another consideration is being efficient with equipment. Try to save carabiners, conserve cordage, and "steal" your partner's gear if they are in need/unable to use. Be prepared to improvise. Probably the most important part is to practice using self-rescue tools regularly. Having an expectation to execute a technical procedure in a stressful rescue situation when you have never done so in any situation before is not realistic.

For other assistance skills to develop seek additional training.

- Pass a knot on a lower.

- Pass a knot on a rappel.

- More complex/powerful haul systems.

- Progressions to baseline with an MBD.

- Ascending without an ABD.

- Other methods to rappel with an injured partner.

CHAPTER 11

Beyond This Text

B eyond this text is a vast world of climbing possibilities. Most conspicuously, taller trad climbs await. This text has endeavored to restrict its content to the skills needed for small climbs, but those climbs undoubtedly beckon bigger climbs, and the skills one hones on a 300-foot cliff can translate into 500-foot cliffs, or even 5,000-foot cliffs. However, with each great leap in adventure, a great leap in risk accompanies one's ambition. We have discussed belaying a leader, and we have discussed belaying a second. So many climbers begin to wonder, "Can the second not belay the leader from a mid-cliff anchor as well as they can from the ground?" They ask, "If I can climb ten single pitch climbs in a day, can I not climb one ten-pitch climb in a day?" These are logical inducements of one's experience and the insight one gains. The answer to each question is the same, incidentally. The answer is, of course you can—but should you?

The multipitch climbing team must know all the skills we've discussed in this book, but they must also be acutely aware of how to prepare further and research bigger climbs. They must know how to construct anchors that can withstand an upward pull. They must be prepared to protect a leader from factor 2 fall forces by using omnidirectional protection strategies immediately off the belay, or use the anchor's components or the anchor itself as protection or a fixed point belay. They must be prepared to improvise rescue

**Suggested trad climbing progression
before attempting an actual lead:**

1. Review and refine toproping, sport climbing, artificial protection, lead belaying, and all the skills relevant to trad climbing, and get feedback when appropriate.
2. Learn to clean protection; follow an experienced leader on many pitches.
3. Learn trad clipping, runner craft, and ropework.
4. Learn to build and utilize trad anchors.
5. Mock lead under the protection of a separate toprope belay—get feedback.
6. Repeat.
7. Consider practicing managed falls on artificial protection.

Once leading, you should:

1. Self-assess: Do you need coursework or instruction from an AMGA professional? Are you ready to lead?
2. Lead "easy" single pitch climbs well below your sport climbing limit.
3. Lead harder single pitch climbs.
4. Try to onsight (to lead a climb without any falls, and without any prior knowledge) or flash (to lead a climb without any falls, and with some knowledge, but no previous attempts).
5. Set your eyes on multipitch climbing.

systems that are more complex because the ground gets farther and farther away as the team climbs higher and higher.

We would never discourage a climber from seeking adventure, but our text strives to impress each reader with the value that great adventure is imprudent if the associated risks cannot be responsibly managed. This book does not entirely prepare a reader for multipitch climbing. But, like the toproper prepares to sport climb, and the sport climber prepares to climb trad, the trad climber can prepare to climb multipitch, ice, or mountains. There are so many vast and wonderful endeavors to sample.

Hopefully there is a flowering to-do list in every aspiring climber's mind. The foundations of protection, anchors, and the host of technical skills required to manage risk on smaller cliffs are intriguing and exciting. We recommend the following progression for sport climbing to traditional lead climbing:

1. Take personal responsibility for what you know and what you don't know yet. Honestly self-assess your skills. Ensure your toproping, sport climbing, and protection skills are sharp and mastered—practice until you own them (see *Climbing: Gym to Rock*, *Climbing: Toproping to Sport*, *Climbing: Knots*, and *Climbing: Protection* texts). You should be able to move with ease around a toproping or sport climbing crag, maximizing your day and managing risk. You do not need a more experienced person around for these disciplines.

2. Spend time with an AMGA-certified instructor or guide, or work with a mentor. For many, mock leading (practice leading with a separate toprope belay) is a great way to start. Do some seconding

and take notes and photos. Seek feedback from a professional-level mentor or instructor on protection, anchoring, and ropework. Look for an affirmation that your leads won't be prematurely undertaken.

Practicel Climbers rehearse mock leading and mock lead belaying all under the protection of a toprope and a belay.

3. Be the second. Go trad climbing outside with an experienced trad leader. Second and support them all day. Be a belayer for them for a day. Help make the Big Plan, help do research, ask lots of questions.

4. Be the leader. Research, pack, and go. Do your homework. Learn all about the trad crags you want to visit, the rock, the first ascents, the flora and fauna, the landowners, and the local climbing coalition and its leadership. Get the gear you need. Learn all about the routes you want to do. Go trad climbing with people with at least equal experience. Follow best practices outlined in this text—trad climb. Repeat this a number of times.

5. Once you've been the leader on a handful of outings, start exploring and challenging yourself further. You know you have arrived when your trad climbing ability starts to approach your sport climbing ability.

6. When more complex objectives beckon, don't dive right in. Be as thorough and procedural as you were with all the other disciplines of climbing. Seek a new mentor, a new instructor, and a new text.

Have fun out there and be careful.

An engaged trad climber in action.

About the Authors

Nate Fitch is a faculty member in the renowned Outdoor Education Department at the University of New Hampshire specializing in climbing courses/programing and is the director of the Gass Climbing Center. He is an AMGA–certified single-pitch instructor and apprentice rock guide who is also active in providing AMGA instructor programs as a climbing wall instructor provider and a single-pitch instructor assistant provider. He has climbed and instructed climbing all over the United States and abroad. Nate is the owner of Pawtuckaway Climbing School and Mountain Guides. He lives with his wife and two kids in Durham, New Hampshire.

Ron Funderburke is an AMGA–certified rock guide. He is the AMGA SPI Discipline Coordinator, the education manager at the American Alpine Club, and a senior climbing specialist with the North Carolina Outward Bound School. Ron lives in Golden, Colorado, with his wife and sons.